Mad About Money

Mad About Money

Managing Finances (and Life) with ADHD

Maddy Alexander-Grout

WILEY

Registered Offices
John Wiley & Sons, Inc., 111 River Street, Hoboken, NJ 07030, USA
John Wiley & Sons Ltd, New Era House, 8 Oldlands Way, Bognor Regis, West Sussex, PO22 9NQ, UK

For details of our global editorial offices, customer services, and more information about Wiley products visit us at www.wiley.com.

The manufacturer's authorized representative according to the EU General Product Safety Regulation is Wiley-VCH GmbH, Boschstr. 12, 69469 Weinheim, Germany, e-mail: Product_Safety@wiley.com.

Library of Congress Cataloging-in-Publication Data is Available:

ISBN 9781394299720 (Paperback)
ISBN 9781394299744 (ePDF)
ISBN 9781394299737 (ePub)

Cover Design: Wiley
Cover Images: © G C Sabini-Roberts, © nupixel/Shutterstock, © elchinarts/Shutterstock, © Maman/Adobe Stock
Author Photo: © Katie Needle

Set in 12/18 pts and Avenir LT Std by Straive, Chennai, India.

SKY10099970_031325

For my Bear, Ben and Harri.

Contents

Foreword

Like Maddy, I wasn't diagnosed with ADHD until much later in life – I was 42 when I received my diagnosis. With all of the recent awareness online particularly towards women's ADHD, I knew that's exactly what I had been experiencing all my life but I was still shocked when I was diagnosed. Learning how to manage my ADHD but also finally being on the correct medication rather than having a ton of antidepressants thrown down my neck, it's safe to say that it's been life-changing.

Like Maddy, I also went the long way around when it came to getting a diagnosis, which involved making some pretty bad decisions in my life in my 20s. You may have even read about it in the papers at some point in the early 2000s!

I developed an unhealthy relationship with alcohol, I got into a lot of debt, I had broken relationships and a 19-year battle with my mental health. It was as though I had become a 90s popstar cliché! In

2020, I had, had enough! It was time to completely change my lifestyle. I quit drinking, went plant-based and took up running, which was the beginning of my journey to a happier and healthier life.

Changing my lifestyle meant I could manage my mood so much better – I had more energy and had more clarity. I wasn't chasing quick fixes from alcohol and food anymore and having the extreme highs and the brutal lows. However, I did notice, if I didn't work out I felt empty and low, frustrated, extremely scatty and generally a bit lost, just like I had done all my life. Therefore, I kept throwing myself into running challenges and gym classes, which in turn was having a detrimental effect as I was often ending up with burnout.

When I started perimenopause, all my ADHD symptoms highlighted, even when I was running and going to the gym. I spent a year shaming myself and beating myself up for my mishaps and not being able to regulate my moods. I went for blood test after blood test to see if this was the menopause, but every time it came back that there were no signs of hormone change. Just as Maddy did, I disappeared into hyperfocus-fuelled online research and discovered an incredible community of people with ADHD – thank goodness there are people out there sharing their stories.

This meant I could finally get the diagnosis I had frankly needed all my life! When the psychiatrist announced the words 'I can confirm you have inattentive ADHD', I went through a short period of being angry that this hadn't been picked up sooner. Especially considering I had been in and out of my doctors for 19 years trying to understand my anxiety and depression, desperately trying to get them to understand that antidepressants weren't right and was it something else I was experiencing? It's even come to light that my ADHD gets worse when I'm hormonal and this can be the case for many women – it was horrific when I was pregnant and postnatal.

I am passionate about people getting diagnosed early, to save the pain, confusion, shame and heartache I endured for 42 years. Through this book and her own content, Maddy is on a similar mission.

We both know what it feels like to feel as though you don't fit into the world as everyone else sees it. We know how damaging that can be for your self-esteem and confidence. And we want other people to get the support they need to embrace their ADHD traits and live amazing lives where they work with their brains, not against them.

This book isn't just for people who have ADHD, or suspect they do. It's also for anyone who lives with or knows someone with ADHD. You'll learn a lot about how to support an ADHDer in your life by reading this, and you'll get a much better understanding of the condition and all its nuances.

So, read Maddy's story. She has shared an incredibly honest, open and brave account of her life with you in these pages. Along the way, she shares a host of valuable tips and advice to help you on your own journey to better understanding and managing your ADHD.

I only wish there had been books like this available to me when I was younger.

Singer, Actress and Performance Coach
Suzanne Shaw

Acknowledgements

For my family and friends who have supported me unwavering through my life, my diagnosis, my permanent oops mode* and writing this book.

For my **Invisible To Influential** members who cheerlead me in everything I do.

For the specialists who helped me with tips, and generously contributed their advice. Without them, this book wouldn't have been possible.

Thanks to Marie Edwards, who created the full-page illustrations in this book, G Sabini-Roberts, who is responsible for the logo, image and cover designs, and Katie Needle who took the fabulous photo of me that's included on the back cover.

And for every single one of my followers on **Mad About Money Official** who give me my daily dopamine hits.

Preface

Hi, I'm Maddy and I am a money, business and social media coach for people who have invisible conditions. I spent my life feeling like a failed horse when, really, I was a beautifully normal zebra. I just didn't know for the first 38 years of my life. I felt like I did everything wrong all the time.

I have what I describe as a fruit bowl of neurodivergent conditions:

- ADHD: attention deficit hyperactivity disorder, which is characterised by patterns of inattention, impulsivity and sometimes hyperactivity that interfere with daily life.

- Autism: a spectrum disorder which affects how you communicate, interact socially and process information.

- Dyslexia: this primarily affects reading and language processing, making it difficult to spell, read or recognise words accurately and fluently.

- Dyspraxia: this affects motor coordination and planning leading to challenges with physical tasks and sometimes speech.

- Dyscalculia: this affects your ability to understand and work with numbers, often impacting mathematical reasoning and basic calculations including money.

- Dysgraphia: this involves difficulties with writing and affects handwriting, spelling and organisation.

- Oh, and discombobulation (OK I made that one up).

I also have an autoimmune disease (a condition where the immune system mistakenly attacks the body's own cells and tissues), I'm perimenopausal (the transitional phase before menopause when a woman's body begins to undergo hormonal changes leading to the end of her reproductive years), I have PMDD (premenstrual disorder – a severe form of premenstrual syndrome and a chronic condition that causes intense physical, emotional and behavioural symptoms in the luteal phase of the menstrual cycle), and half the time I don't know if I'm coming or going. I have bright hair, sometimes it's rainbow, sometimes pink, sometimes blue. The only thing I change more is my underwear!

I'm always the one doing crazy stuff; starting a new business, dancing on a bar on a night out, and accidentally going to a fetish club. Yeah, that happened once! I'm going to tell you my story.

Strap in! It's bumpy. I am also going to talk to you about how my neurodivergent conditions have shown up in my life. I was diagnosed with most of them when I was 38; I'm 40 as I write this! And it's eye-opening. Before my diagnosis, I didn't feel like I fit into this world. Now, I absolutely love my life and my brain.

I'm a huge music fan and all the chapters are dedicated to the songs that remind me of times in my life. Everyone has a soundtrack to their lives and a mixtape that captures their personality. The titles for these chapters are part of mine. If you want to listen along you can download the playlist from Spotify here:

Those of us with ADHD often listen to the same song on repeat because this helps us focus and maintain our energy, as well as giving us an immediate dopamine hit. A familiar song provides predictability and control in our environment, which creates a sense of security and can be really grounding. I've certainly found that listening to a familiar song on repeat helps me get into a flow state and avoid decision fatigue and procrastafaffing*.

This book was produced in collaboration with Write Business Results Limited. For more information on their business book and marketing services, please visit www.writebusinessresults.com or contact the team via info@writebusiness results.com.

Trigger warning: This book contains my story, which includes sexual assault, rape and suicidal thoughts. I also talk about prenatal and postpartum depression, and postpartum psychosis. It's important that we talk about these difficult topics, but if any of those are too much for you, just skip the relevant sections and read the rest. There's a trigger warning in the relevant chapter too, just so you know when the hard stuff is coming up.

Introduction

It's important to know that this book isn't just about money. It's about life, relationships, business, family and more. It's my ADHD journey.

But although I have ADHD, this is not my defining characteristic as a person. There are many things that make up 'me' – ADHD and my other conditions are just a few of them. I'm also a mother, a wife, a sister, a daughter, a business owner, a *TikTok* creator and so much more. So, while I own my neurodivergent conditions, they don't define me.

That said, they have had an impact on me my whole life. A big part of my story is about money. No matter how you look at it, money makes the world go round, and whether you have none of it or lots of it, money affects everything around you.

There are usually two types of people when it comes to ADHD and money. The people who hyperfocus know exactly what they are doing and are living life on full blast. And the people who spend dopamine get caught with ADHD tax, struggle to manage money, never have any of it, can't hold down a job and are always looking down the back of the sofa to find a coin for the supermarket trolley. I was the latter.

If you have neurodivergent conditions and money problems, you are not broken. It's really hard to manage money as a neurodivergent, especially when you don't know you are. This is a story of me and undiagnosed ADHD, how I got into £40,000 of debt – and how I got myself out of it. I don't hold back. I talk about my failed relationships, my failed businesses and my messed-up life before realising I was neurodivergent. It's also a story of how my neurodivergent conditions have shown up for me over the last 40 years, warts and all.

I have to tell you early on, I'm an oversharer. I'm about to get mega vulnerable with you guys. In fact, writing this book feels like I'm getting naked in front of not just you, but an entire stadium full of people! I had this realisation while at a Foo Fighters gig at Wembley, where I was trying to get an endorsement for this book from Dave Grohl (spoiler alert, he didn't get back to me).

This book will make you laugh, it may make you cry, it will teach you to be better with your money and neurodivergent conditions. If you don't have money problems, you will still find this book useful. I hope it will inspire you to achieve your goals and realise that if I can start smashing life, you can too.

I have what I like to call a fruit bowl of neurodivergent conditions, but I haven't always known about them. Despite the word money being in the title of this book, it is not a boring money book. Far from it. It will help you to be better with money. It may even help you to start a business. It will definitely help you if you have or suspect you have a neurodivergent condition.

I'm hoping you will relate to it and learn a thing or two on how to thrive when you are neurodivergent whether it's with money, business or life. Because this book is written for people who have (or suspect they have) ADHD, I have written it in a way that either you can hyperfocus on it and read the whole thing, or you can just pick out the tips you need by flicking through. Whichever way you do it I hope you enjoy it and find it useful.

There are tips scattered throughout the book and you might notice some of them seem to be the same. That's because sometimes we need repetition for the message to get through.

I've also reached out to a whole host of experts in different areas, and they have kindly provided tips and advice specifically for this book. I'm not an expert in everything, and I've found other people's support invaluable on my journey, so I wanted to share that with you too.

This book comes with a warning: I don't sugarcoat things, and sometimes the only way to describe

life's chaos is with a well-placed f-bomb or two.
I know that navigating business, money, and life's
struggles can get messy, frustrating, and downright
ridiculous. So, to keep things real – and a bit
colorful – I've put together a 'fuck glossary'.

Consider it your go-to translation guide for all the
creative, sweary language that captures the ups,
downs and WTFs we face along the way. Hopefully
it'll make you laugh too! So, when you see a word
or phrase pop up followed by a *, flip to the
glossary and get the lowdown. Think of it as a
f**k-filled dictionary that keeps things interesting
and reminds you that it's OK to embrace the messy,
unfiltered journey.

And man has my journey been messy at times. It's
also been traumatic in places, so be aware that I
will talk about difficult topics, including sexual
assault, rape, depression and suicidal thoughts
throughout this book.

Chapter 1

Just a Girl

> **Just a Girl** *by No Doubt – from their album*
> **Tragic Kingdom**
>
> This song is super powerful, and it makes me feel empowered, it made me feel like I wasn't just a silly little girl.

Before we get to the age where I was rocking out to No Doubt, I'll tell you a bit about my childhood, which, in all honesty, was great. I grew up in a quiet village called Over Wallop. It's in the middle of nowhere, and it didn't have much in the way of amenities – a little shop with a post office, a phone box and a cricket field.

Village life was far from riveting. There were no bright lights or big cities in my childhood.

My parents were loving and my sister Rebecca and I never went without, although I think at times they did struggle for money. My mum worked in IT and my dad was self-employed, and they both worked really hard.

My dad owned his own business and worked as a rubber merchant at a rubber factory where they made products like matting, hoses and gaskets. Unfortunately, kids hear rubber and think 'condoms', so I often got teased about it. Our surname, Comrie, didn't help either – apparently it sounds like condom, so I was given the nickname 'Maddy Condom' around the age of nine, which is pretty scarring for a child, even though at that age I had no real idea of what a condom was!

I know that compared to so many people we were really privileged. We lived in a bungalow on a little hill next door to a farm. We had a huge garden with loads of space to run around.

My parents each had their own cars because they worked in different locations and, as I'm sure you can imagine, a village as small as ours didn't have a particularly regular bus service.

That's a broad picture of what my really early life looked like, but what was I like?

WHO AM I?

I wasn't a particularly hyper kid, not a problem child. I did have loads of energy and I bounced from one activity to another. I think by the time I was about eight years old, I had tried every hobby and musical instrument that my parents could afford to let me try.

Flute, recorder, violin, bass guitar, piano, clarinet – you name it, I'd probably had some lessons and then moved on before making much progress. But my hobbies weren't restricted to music. I also tried trampolining, judo, gymnastics, pottery and horse riding. None of them stuck. I just changed my mind all the time.

My parents were amazing and were very understanding about my many hobbies. They worked hard to provide for me and my sister, they were present, they were loving and they supported us in every way possible. The thing is, like many parents of children in the 1980s and 1990s, attention deficit hyperactivity disorder (ADHD) wasn't on their radar, and it certainly wasn't a condition that people expected girls to have.

I doubt it ever occurred to my parents that I might have ADHD or any other condition that I talk about in this book. If you're reading this and you're a similar age to me, it's highly likely that your parents were in the same situation. There just wasn't the research or information available to educate us even 20 years ago that we have access to now. ADHD was just for naughty little boys.

It also has nothing to do with how you are parented or how much screen time you give your kids, I barely watched TV as a kid.

When I was growing up, ADHD and autism were just not common especially in girls. It wasn't my parent's fault in any way that I wasn't diagnosed with these conditions when I was younger. That's also true of your parents. After all, how were they supposed to know when I didn't know myself? The doctors didn't even know. Society didn't know.

Enable, Don't Label

If you suspect your child is neurodivergent, I'd advise you to get a diagnosis earlier rather than later. This isn't about labelling your child as one thing or another, but about helping them learn about themselves and how their brains work earlier in life and providing tools that can support them. In doing so, you're enabling them to succeed and navigate the world.

The key to any conversation about neurodivergent conditions, especially with children, is to help them understand that neurodiversity isn't wrong; it's just a difference. The way I like to think of it is that there are lots of different brains they just approach the world in a different way.

What it really comes down to is that the sooner a child can get a diagnosis, the sooner you as a parent can help them understand their brain and find their own 'normal'. According to ADHD Aware, it's thought that 15% of people in the UK are neurodivergent.[1]

Based on the size of the UK population as I write this, that's over 10 million of us. Imagine the whole population of London, plus about another half a million people. That is a lot of people! So, although it might feel challenging and lonely at times, you are certainly not alone if you are neurodivergent.

> If you suspect your child has ADHD, don't panic! This doesn't mean that they're damaged and there are many successful people in this world with ADHD – like Richard Branson and Simone Biles. Your child has incredible potential. There are more tips on what to do if your child has ADHD later in the book.

One of the reasons I think it's best to get an ADHD diagnosis as early as possible for your child is because this will allow you to help them in all areas of their lives, not just at school.

Most of us don't get any formal 'money education', ADHD or not. When you have ADHD, this doesn't help, as it can mean that you have a tendency to approach your finances differently.

---

[1] ADHD Aware (2023) *What is Neurodiversity – ADHD Aware.* https://adhdaware.org.uk/what-is-adhd/neurodiversity-and-other-conditions/

When I was growing up, my parents didn't really talk openly about money, but I still wanted to know everything about it. I played with money from an early age. I had a post office set, a bank, an office and even a National Lottery (which was actually just a bingo machine). It was fun pretending I had won the lottery.

Shameless Plug

Look at money books for kids that are available. I've written one called *That's My Money*, which is illustrated by the fabulous Chris Dixon.

The real-life money I was given was always spent on toys, books or games. Whatever my latest hyperfocus was, my money was heading its way.

My sister Bex and I were given £2 a week pocket money. My parents told me about saving, but I was always more interested in spending it. My parents taught me how you earn, spend and save money. However, I found numbers and counting really difficult. I think what they taught me just went in one ear and out the other.

I think I learned better through play, so I recommend any parents who want to teach their kids about money use play to do so. You can pick up pretend money in bargain basement stores, or even give them an old card of yours, so you can show them how cash and cards work.

I also recommend money games like Monopoly – the house prices might be massively off, but it's a great way to teach kids some basic money rules.

My best friend when I was at primary school was a girl named Alex. She became my hyperfocus – I wanted everything she had. So, we both had Cabbage Patch dolls (remember them?!). I wasn't sure they were my thing, but Alex liked them, so I did too. I even started dressing like her.

If Alex got something, I immediately wanted it, but I wasn't always allowed. My parents didn't earn that much, and while we always had enough money for food and essentials, when it came to toys, I couldn't just ask and expect to be given what I wanted.

That meant I waited eagerly for birthdays and Christmas. Several of my aunts and uncles would send me money in a card – the best present. This was where my obsession with buying things came from. To me, money bought me the things I wanted and therefore money equalled happiness. Even though my parents tried to encourage me to save, I would always spend whatever money I had.

NAVIGATING SCHOOL

My grandparents paid for me to go to private school until I was seven years old, but I changed schools a lot when I was younger. The first school, Marsh Court, was where I got my phobia of peas from. They're horrible things!

They pop when you get through the shell, and they make me feel violently ill. I hate everything about peas: the taste, the smell, the texture, even the way they look. So, I used to stuff them into my cheek like a deranged hamster and spit them out in the toilet. We weren't allowed to leave the table to go and play until we had finished everything on our plates.

I found that being forced to eat something I couldn't handle from a sensory perspective was incredibly traumatic. But I had to face peas at every meal at school for a year. In case you're wondering, I still hate peas, they are green devils disguised as vegetables!

Neurodivergent Conditions and Food

People with neurodivergent conditions, but particularly children, are more sensitive to the textures of food and to other sensory inputs associated with eating. We are also more likely to experience sensory sensitivity or sensory overload, which means that we get overwhelmed by sensory stimuli.[2]

If you're a parent to a neurodivergent child, you'll probably relate to this. The best piece of advice I can give you, based on my childhood experiences

(continued)

---

[2] *What Is Sensory Sensitivity? | Neurodivergence Glossary* (no date). https://www.healthyyoungminds.com/learn-about/sensory-sensitivity/

and now my experience as a parent, is not to force-feed your children anything. Let them try new foods, but don't push it if they don't like them, or just mince them up so tiny they can't even see!

Let's be honest, none of us have come to like a food just because we were force-fed it as children!

I also remember that I regularly peed my pants at that school. I was four years old, but the toilets were outside and there were spiders in them. I was so scared of the spiders that if I needed to go, I would pee my pants rather than going into a spider-filled cupboard!

Just like with food, children and adults with ADHD and other neurodivergent conditions tend to feel emotions more intensely than others. So, these experiences at my first school were forcing me way out of my comfort zone and inducing anxiety.

I also remember being told off because I put glue in another girl's hair. My intention was to see if it made her hairstyle better, but I hadn't thought through any of the consequences of my actions. Children with ADHD are impulsive, and that's just one example of a reflex reaction. Of course, I got into trouble for that – the other girl's parents weren't impressed!

I was only at that first school for a year before I moved to Holmewood House School in Salisbury. The great thing about this school was that I had two friends,

Alex and Eliza. Eliza's parents were a lord and lady. They had a swimming pool, tennis courts and a nanny.

I remember playing at Eliza's house once and we made cookies. They smelled so good! We ate them all. Apparently, that wasn't what we were supposed to do and her nanny shouted at us. But I had trouble controlling my impulses when it came to sugar – another common trait among children with ADHD. The nanny said I was a bad influence, and I wasn't allowed back to play after that.

Alex, on the other hand, was my best friend. I would spend as much time as I could with her and I got very jealous of anyone else she was friends with. I now know she was my hyperfocus, my person. I have always had a person who gets all of me, even if they don't really want it! Neurotypical people don't tend to understand this, so I often felt like people couldn't handle me.

Alex lived around the corner from me, so we used to walk to each other's houses. We were allowed to do this even as young as six or seven, as long as we did three rings on the phone when we got there. Of course, I pretty much always forgot to make the call, and my mum would come storming round or phone up Alex's mum to check if I was there.

My next school was Stroud, about which I remember very little. But I do remember the other students often calling me 'stupid'. There was a long list of criticisms and digs: 'She can't read! She copies stuff off the board wrong! It's like she can't see it. She never sits still, she is always squirming and fidgeting like she has ants in her pants!'

My mum had no idea what to do with me, but she thought if I wasn't seeing the board well enough that I might need glasses. I liked the idea of glasses! They sounded cool. I could get pink ones.

So, I went to the optician. I was clever. I knew I could see fine, but I just couldn't read the letters in the right order. I wanted to be different and get glasses – and I did. They were pink with a little diamond in each corner. Of course, they didn't help me to see what was on the board and they didn't help me to copy any better. My mum was upset that the other students kept calling me stupid, and the fees were expensive, so my parents decided to move me to a state primary school.

I learnt some valuable lessons from my time at those different private schools. First, forcing kids to eat something, or do something, isn't going to make them like it. Second, as parent (and adult), I have learnt that putting something nice on a pedestal, like going out to play or pudding, encourages children to rebel and makes talking about it taboo.

I rebelled. I wasn't allowed chocolate and sweets, so I would eat them behind my parents' backs and, as you'll hear a bit later in my story, this led to an eating disorder.

Being forced to run during physical education lessons throughout my childhood has created a lifelong hatred of running in me. When we're young, and particularly around primary school age, our fears, beliefs, ideals and value systems are constructed and shaped by what happens in our lives. So, if you drive kids to do things they hate, all you're doing is setting them up to hate that activity during adulthood. I later learned I was dyspraxic which was why my coordination left a lot to be desired.

I started a new primary school in year three, which was when I started to work out how I learned. I loved music, I loved art and I also loved times tables. I was always the fastest in my class at times tables, but only because I listened to them as music, and somehow they sunk into my brain. I didn't know how to multiply them, but I learnt patterns through sound.

It didn't take my mum long to realise that the best way for me to learn was through tapes! Remember them? You could fast-forward, rewind, press play or stop. We had music, educational and story tapes. I remember that I listened to **The Ugly Duckling** on repeat to the point that I could recite it word for word.

The fact that my mum noticed that tapes were a good way for me to learn shows what a great parent she was. If your child has a neurodivergent condition, explore different ways to help them

(continued)

learn because often it's not that kids are stupid, but simply that they take information on board in different ways. When you find the way that works for your child, you'll see a big difference in how much and how quickly they learn.

When I wasn't learning, I was playing chess with my dad or had my head deep inside a book. I was reading books for 10–11 year olds by the time I was seven. My dad started taking me to the library every weekend, which became our little ritual. We would also do the food shopping while we were out. I would be in charge of the list and finding deals. There were signs I was going to be a money saver. Just a shame I didn't start sooner!

Go Shopping Together

Take your kids shopping, online or in-store, especially if they're neurodivergent. It teaches money skills, but only if it doesn't overwhelm you. They will learn valuable money skills, if you can cope with them in the supermarket.

I never became a saver during my childhood – there were just too many shiny, exciting things to spend my money on. I remember when I discovered the TV show **Gladiators,** where regular contestants would compete in all kinds of physical challenges against the 'gladiators'. I loved it and watched it every weekend without fail.

I started collecting **Gladiators** stickers – if you were also a child of the 1980s and 1990s, you'll probably remember that there was a sticker book for everything. But I didn't just collect the stickers, I wanted all of them. I would do chores like emptying the dishwasher and washing the car to earn my own money so I could buy more packs of stickers. I never saved. Every single penny I had went on my latest obsession. The shiny stickers made me so happy.

Another obsession of mine at this time was Pogs, which were like round cardboard milk caps that you could stack and build a game out of (another 1990s throwback!). Just like with the **Gladiators** stickers, I wanted to have all the Pogs. If I wasn't buying **Gladiators** stickers, I was buying Pogs, and I had hundreds of them.

Needs vs Wants

It is really valuable to talk to your children about needs vs wants when they are young so that they are better able to make the distinction when they get older.

My new teacher told my mum that I was hyperactive. She said I was always on the go, and recommended I get checked out by the doctor.

'She is allergic to E-numbers, Mrs Comrie', the doctor told my mum.

'What do you mean?' mum asked.

'She has an artificial colouring allergy: sweets, pro-cessed food, fizzy pop', the doctor explained in a matter-of-fact way.

No one questioned the fact that I had never been exposed to this type of food before. I had been at a private school for three years, eating what seemed like nothing except meat, potatoes and vegetables. We never even got pudding apart from semolina – and that stuff was gross, hardly a sugary treat.

But this diagnosis of an allergy to E-numbers was really common in the 1980s and early 1990s, especially for girls who were considered 'hyper'. Let's be honest, so many kids in the 1980s and 1990s were 'allergic' to E-numbers that they had to discontinue blue Smarties (a sugar-coated chocolate sweet for anyone not in the UK)!

So, that doctor's diagnosis meant that I never had any sugar or processed foods. I was the weird kid at birth-day parties who couldn't have the Panda Pop or the jelly. I couldn't have the weird and wonderful things the other kids were given at parties.

I would get really frustrated that all of the other kids were allowed the treats and I was given nothing. The truth is, like many other kids who were similarly deprived, I didn't have an artificial colouring allergy at all. I had ADHD and I just didn't know it – and neither did anyone else.

Gems of Wisdom

- ADHD means that our brains work differently to people who are neurotypical. Take the time to understand how that affects the way you learn and approach the world.

- Getting an ADHD diagnosis for yourself or your child can give you access to support and help you learn new ways of managing life.

- Educate your kids about money from an early age. Find ways to involve them in finances around the house, such as by taking them shopping and encouraging them to save at least some of their pocket money.

- If you have a child with ADHD, be kind to yourself. It can be challenging to parent a kid with ADHD, so make sure you look after yourself as well as looking after them.

Chapter 2

The Kids Aren't Alright

> **The Kids Aren't Alright** *by The Offspring –*
> *from their album* **Americana**
>
> I had a hard time at school and this song helped
> me to just carry on.

Primary school was a piece of cake, but when I started secondary school, I realised on my first day that I was going to struggle. The school was so big and there were so many people. There were so many options, which confused me – how to wear my hair, what pencil case to have, how much to roll up my skirt, who to hang out with, etc.

In primary school, it was so easy; I just arrived, and everything was there for me. There was one class where everyone just played together, but now I had to think about so much more. I had a different book for every class, a homework diary and I had to move rooms for every lesson.

There were also **so many boys**!! I felt really over-whelmed, and I had no idea why. Everything was new and my brain was working overtime. That all made me feel nervous. When I'm nervous, I overtalk, so people quickly realised I was the chatty one.

This is quite common among those of us with ADHD, and in some ways, it can make it easier for us to make friends, because we're very talkative and sociable. However, we have to balance that, because it is also easy for us to overcompensate for our anxiety, overshare and, in doing so, repel people.

But when I started at secondary school, my talkative nature really helped. My first friends were Rachel and Fuzzy we bonded instantly. Having new friends was really exciting and the first two years at secondary school flew by.

I was usually the one in class swinging on my chair, writing notes or whispering behind the teacher's back. That's not because I was naughty, but because I was restless. I even enjoyed being sent out of class because it gave me an excuse to move around and watch what was going on in the corridors. The school bell used to scare the living daylights out of me.

It was so loud, and I didn't like loud unexpected noises.

Although I had Rachel and Fuzzy, I never really found my place. I sort of hang out with everyone. There were the usual groups in school – the smokers, the mean girls, the cool kids and the 'normal' kids, the geeks. I wasn't in any particular crowd.

I shifted from group to group and found that I fell out with people because I overshared or interrupted. I remember that at this age, I was just excited about what I wanted to say, so I'd talk over someone else. But then everyone would glare at me because I came across as rude. Oh and I was WEIRD!

Why Do People with ADHD Overshare?

- We can struggle to know what is and isn't appropriate.

- We can often be socially awkward, so we try to fill gaps in the conversation.

- We are often impulsive, so we can blurt stuff out that we don't mean to.

- We want to feel liked, and oversharing can sometimes give us a feeling of connection.

My advice to anyone, of any age, who recognises these traits in themselves is to learn about ADHD, watch *TikTok* clips, especially mine!

The more you learn, the more you can understand how your brain works, and knowledge is power.

At school these days, because there's a lot more education and awareness of neurodivergent conditions, I think it's probably easier to find other people who understand your condition.

But my experience at school after the first couple of years, even with best friends like Rachel and Fuzzy, was that I just didn't feel like I fitted in. There were two girls in particular who were really mean to me. I nicknamed them Katty and Malice. I'd go home and cry every day. Often, I'd tell my mum that I was going to bed early just so I could be on my own.

This was when my dopamine hunting started – which I'll talk more about shortly – which I used to fill a void.

If you've been through, or are going through, something similar, my advice is to get to know who you really are and learn to love that person – easier said than done, I know! Once you know who you are, it'll be much easier to find your people. If you can, surround yourself with people who like and understand you.

What I've learned is that it's exhausting trying to please people all the time. There are so many better outlets for your energy than trying to fit in – I wish I'd known that sooner.

Why Do Kids with ADHD Struggle to Fit In?

- We can be perceived as rude if we interrupt or talk about ourselves a lot.

- We often have special hobbies or interests that aren't the same as other people's.

- We struggle with friendships because we have a tendency to focus on one or two people who can feel overwhelmed by us.

- We can be impulsive, which means that we might do the wrong thing socially or be a bit silly.

- We have rejection sensitivity dysphoria (RSD), which means that we often walk on eggshells because we're so desperate to avoid criticism or judgement from others.

BOYS, BOYS, BOYS

I was quite an early developer when it came to fancying boys and I used to talk about them *a lot*. I had one boyfriend, David, which lasted about three weeks, and then another. I used to get bored quickly and then move on (or I got dumped for being annoying).

Looking back, I can see that because not all of my friends were at the same stage as me, they probably found my constant talk about boys annoying. But I didn't really think about the people around me back then, or what it was appropriate to talk about. Instead of observing a situation and taking it in, I'd just rhino in* and blurt something out. At this age, what I'd blurt out was almost always about whichever boy I fancied most that day.

The thing was fancying boys wasn't new to me. I remember telling everyone I loved Simon, my first crush, when I was about seven years old. My world revolved around him. I thought about marrying him, day and night. But my love was very much unrequited. The presents I bought him always went in the bin, and he'd return the love notes I sent him in the shape of a paper aeroplane.

People who are neurotypical might read that and remember also sending unrequited love notes to someone in their class, or fixating on a boy and telling people they loved them. They can absolutely experience similar symptoms, but when you have ADHD, these feelings are even more intense.

I would literally become obsessed with a particular boy and my whole focus would be on him. I'd think about him 24/7. He'd be in my dreams. My thoughts about him would distract me in class and even impact my schoolwork. Those of us with

(continued)

neurodivergent conditions often struggle with emotional regulation, and this can mean that our emotions overwhelm us. This is particularly true when it comes to rejection.

In my first year at secondary school, Simon was long forgotten. My big crush was a boy who lived in Wallop named Leon Fudge. He had jet black hair, olive skin and was a bit cheeky. I think my first taste of RSD was when my dad found out I fancied Leon and over the dinner table started taking the piss out of me for liking a boy.

I was 12 years old, I had just started my period and I was hormonal. You get the idea. My dad didn't mean anything by it – he was just teasing – but I felt horrible. The worst moment was when I thought he had stopped. I said something (I don't remember what) and his reply was, 'Don't fudge the issue'. He smiled, but I remember going bright red, and wishing my chair would sink into the ground. I felt sick in the pit of my stomach.

What Is RSD?

RSD – or rejection sensitivity dysphoria – is a specific ADHD trait. When you have RSD, you're more sensitive to criticism and judgement. This doesn't even have to be genuine criticism; you can also

(continued)

experience RSD when you perceive that you're being criticised, judged or feel like someone doesn't like you for some reason.

It can be experienced as severe mental and/or physical discomfort or pain, which means that it can strike at any time. It can lead to emotional outbursts, impulsive behaviour, rumination and intrusive thoughts.

It often manifests more in internal self-judgement than anything you'd see externally, so it can lead to some very negative self-talk spirals. Sometimes RSD can be triggered when you see someone else doing better than you and wonder why you aren't that person. This isn't like jealousy, because it makes you feel you're not good enough, rather than just wanting what the other person has.

If you find yourself experiencing RSD and feeling as though it derails you, please know you're not alone. Almost 100% of people with ADHD experience RSD,[1] and around 30% of those say that RSD is the most challenging aspect of their ADHD, even though it's not one of the diagnostic criteria.[2]

---

[1] Frye, D. (2024) 'How ADHD Ignites RSD: Meaning & medication solutions', *ADDitude*, 10 July. https://www.additudemag.com/rejection-sensitive-dysphoria-and-adhd/amp/

[2] Rodgers, A.L. (2024) 'New insights into rejection Sensitive Dysphoria', *ADDitude*, 10 July. https://www.additudemag.com/rejection-sensitive-dysphoria-adhd-emotional-dysregulation/amp/

In year eight, we went on a school trip to Normandy. I remember very little about Normandy, but I do remember that I fell in love for the 'first' time, with Gary.

I genuinely have no idea why I fancied Gary. He was pretty short and had that boy band-style floppy hair with an undercut – as did many other boys in the 1990s. He wasn't that special, but I loved him. Or at least I thought I did.

We held hands, but I am not sure we actually ever kissed. He was in year seven, a toy boy! We hung out through the Normandy school trip, and I couldn't stop thinking about how lucky I was. As soon as we got back to school, he dumped me for a girl in the year below. I was heartbroken. Why didn't he want me? Why did he want her?

I cried over a boy I had been 'going out with' for three days as if he had died. What was wrong with me?! I had been rejected **again**! And I had no idea why I was taking it so badly.

What I've since learnt is that this wasn't just RSD; it was also something called 'limerence', which I now realise I've experienced throughout my life. *Limerence* is a term used to describe intense feelings of infatuation. It feels like love, but it isn't. It's an intense emotional feeling where you obsess over a person romantically, even if they have no feelings towards you at all.

Limerence makes you see the person as perfect; you get intrusive thoughts about how much you **need** to be with that person, which makes RSD even worse if they don't want to be with you.

Try to become aware of the sensations you personally experience when RSD flares up, whether it's racing thoughts, a tight chest, pain in your stomach or feeling faint.

Recognising that you're experiencing RSD in the moment can be part of your toolkit to overcome it. If you can 'name it', it can help you feel less as though it's controlling you, even when it feels like it will last forever.

When you have ADHD, your brain can hyperfixate on people as well as things, and this leads to changes in mood, eating, sleeping and basically takes over your life. It's hard to think of any times in my life where I haven't had this intense feeling for people. Now, before you think I am some sort of stalker, I promise I'm not. I didn't rock up outside people's houses or follow them. I had no control over these feelings, and they were mostly unrequited crushes.

This is also another example of my ADHD hyperfocus. When you have ADHD, you can hyperfocus on pretty much anything – food, hobbies or people being just some examples. As an adult, my hyperfocus can also mean that I ruminate over a conversation constantly, worrying about all the things I said or did wrong.

You can't stop yourself developing a hyperfocus, but it is important to be aware when you do. This is particularly important if you hyperfocus on romantic interests, because it can be easy to make an impulsive decision that can ruin a great relationship. I know several people with ADHD who have cheated on their partners purely because they hyperfocused on someone else temporarily and that gave them a dopamine hit.

I've been aware for some time that I'm so in love with my husband that no one else even comes close. I like the attention if someone else flirts with me, but I know that I'm just getting a dopamine hit and that allows me to control my impulses. Being aware of your personal triggers, whatever they might be, is the key to managing your hyperfocus tendencies in a healthy way.

Boys weren't my only love though. In fact, my first big love was music. I used to struggle to get to sleep because I couldn't stop thinking about things, but that all changed the moment I got a tape player. Music helped me switch my brain off and go to sleep.

My godfather, Colin, had given me a tape full of 1980s songs when I was little. I listened to it on repeat for about three years, until I got a CD player. Music always made me feel happy, and if I liked a song, I would listen to it over and over again on repeat until I hated it and never wanted to listen to it ever again.

Even though I loved my tapes, and then my CDs, I couldn't wait to experience live music. I got my first real taste of festivals at Reading in 1998, thanks to my mum, who took me and my friends – I remember seeing Ash, the Deftones, Symposium and Rocket from the Crypt. My mum wanted to see Jimmy Page and Robert Plant; at the time, I thought, 'Who are they?'

Dopamine Hunting

Looking back, I can see that as a child I was always hunting for new dopamine hits, but that escalated on a school trip to Holland in year nine. We were all drinking, smoking and shoplifting – and I'm ashamed to say that I stole too.

The first time I did it, it was a dare. I stole some multi-coloured socks from a shop in Amsterdam. They were so bright that they gave me a dopamine rush, and the buzz I got from not getting caught was insane.

It became a game to see how much I could steal. I knew that this was totally unethical, but I was trying to fit in. Drinking, smoking and stealing seemed to make me cool. I was a rebel – and the boys loved a bad girl! Not that I was the only one misbehaving, we all were.

What we didn't realise when smoking on our balcony was that the deputy head was in the room directly above us. She smelt it, and it wasn't hard for her to work out whose room it was coming from! There was a knock at the door, and I ran into the bathroom, brushed my teeth and sprayed myself with Impulse Vanilla Kisses body spray so I didn't smell! Apparently, that was just enough to avoid having to sleep in a room with the teachers.

My mum was laidback about the whole thing and, in truth, I think she thought it was quite funny. My mum always was the cool mum. She just let me get on with things, but she was always there for me to talk to when I needed to. I picked and chose what I spoke to her about, and I now regret not discussing more of what was happening in my life, given that we're so close as adults.

After Amsterdam, I felt more accepted by the other kids at school. I fitted in mostly by showing off, being the class clown and talking back to the teachers I didn't like. But little did I realise this wasn't going to last.

The Party...

Everyone in our group of friends was invited to a party in a neighbouring village. There was beer, weed and snogging. Only this time, the girls weren't just snogging the boys; we were snogging each other too. I've always been pretty open-minded, curious even and didn't really think anything of it – after all, we were just having fun at a party, right?

The following Monday, someone at school asked me if it was true that the girls had been kissing each other. I said yes. And with that single answer, my whole school experience changed in an instant.

I became the one who 'told'. The other girls who had been at the party stopped talking to me, because other people started to call them 'lemons' – an insulting term for potential queer women back in the day. I had no idea what I'd done that was so wrong. In my mind, someone asked me a question and I just told the truth. I didn't realise it was meant to be a secret; I just opened my big mouth. I didn't see girls kissing girls as a bad thing! And I have done lots of it since!

Later, I started to refer to my inability to hold information in as 'foot-in-mouth disease*'. Sometimes that meant I overshared to fill space in conversation or because I was trying to fit in. Oversharing manifests as situations like telling someone your life story when all they ask is 'How are you?', or telling a story that is completely irrelevant, creating discomfort.

Other times, like this one, being unable to hold information meant that I couldn't keep a secret. This is connected to impulsivity – the words would come out of my mouth before my brain had a chance to think it through. I started to get bullied. All my friends turned their backs on me. I felt so alone I even considered taking my own life.

Although giving away a secret led to extreme consequences at this point in my life, it's worth noting that often other people don't even register that you've overshared. Even if they notice it in the moment, it's very unlikely that they'll remember it later.

The challenge is that when we know we've overshared, we can ruminate on what we've said, which mostly does nothing except lead us down a negative spiral of thoughts. So, if you do overshare, ask yourself the following questions:

- Did anyone die? Almost certainly not, but this helps you put it in context.

- Is it really a massive deal? Or are you making it a bigger deal in your head because you feel bad about what you said?

The more you build up your awareness, the easier you'll find it to catch yourself and not overshare in the first place. So, I know that if someone asks me, 'How are you?' I'll often launch into a detailed response, explaining why I'm feeling how I'm feeling – particularly if I'm feeling low or nervous. But in reality the other person is usually making small talk and I don't have to tell them my life story. I hadn't learnt this when I was a teenager, and it never occurred to me to not tell the truth.

THE FALLOUT

After I revealed what had happened at the party, school was different. Every day, I dreaded going into school. This was when my dopamine hunting took a new turn – or as Rox from ADHD Love calls it 'dopamining', as in mining for dopamine, which I also think is a great term for it.

I started to use my lunch money for vending machine sweets just to try and make myself happy. I developed an eating disorder. If I didn't buy sweets from the vending machine, I'd buy chocolate at the shop. I did this every day.

I would eat it all in secret before my mum came home and would dispose of the evidence in my school bag and put it in the school bin the next day. I had a stash of sweets under my bed. This went on for about a year.

Remember that I'd been told I was 'allergic' to sweets and chocolate and I wasn't allowed them, so I had to keep this a secret. No one knew. My parents had no idea because I did all my bingeing when they were at work.

This was also when I started to buy CDs and clothes because it made me feel good. It took away the pain I had from being bullied at school. It gave me a high. Buying, bingeing and stealing made me feel good. I didn't realise that I was just hunting for dopamine because I had ADHD.

As adults, dopamine hunting can take many forms and not all of them are unhealthy. For example, making money gives me a dopamine hit, but that's a good habit to have. Strong friendships can also give us that hit, again in a healthy way. However, for many ADHD-ers, our dopamine hunting leads to unhealthy habits around spending money, alcohol, sex and drugs.

The best piece of advice I can give you is to learn what your triggers are so that you can manage the unhealthy ones and focus on developing the healthy ways in which you hunt for dopamine.

Finding Healthy Dopamine Habits

The key to managing your hunt for dopamine is to replace your unhealthy habits with healthy ones. I think it's important to assess how healthy or not each thing you do for dopamine is before you try to change anything.

For example, if my child wants to play Roblox to get a dopamine fix, I'm going to let him because that's not causing him or anyone else any harm and I can monitor it to make sure he's getting what he needs. If I were to take that away from him, he'd have a crash which could lead to an unhealthy dopamine habit developing.

Awareness of your dopamine hunting habits is the key to finding healthy ways to get a dopamine fix. One of the things that I find useful to remind myself is that things like drinking alcohol or spending money will only give me a temporary dopamine hit, while the consequences afterwards can be serious and last a lot longer than the seconds or minutes the dopamine is flooding my system.

Our happiness has to come from inside us, not from external things – whether that's shopping, having sex, drinking alcohol, smoking or anything else. The only way we can make ourselves happier is by getting to know ourselves better and really paying attention to what our triggers are.

What I can tell you is that switching from unhealthy to healthy habits is not a quick fix – as you'll learn through the rest of my story. What I've found works for me is to find a healthy habit to replace the unhealthy one with, but first I needed to really examine my relationship with each of my dopamine hunting habits so that I could understand what was driving it and also learn whether it was something I could keep doing but perhaps just less frequently.

◆ Gems of Wisdom

- Oversharing is common when you have ADHD. If you overshare, don't worry. Often other people won't remember what you said. Just build your awareness about what you say when, and see if there are any situations that trigger oversharing for you. What can you do to rein yourself in?

- Silence is golden. Remember that you don't have to fill every silence by saying something.

- Get to know how hyperfocus and RSD show up for you. Be aware of your personal triggers around hyperfocus so you can manage them in a healthy way.

- Pay attention to how you hunt for dopamine hits. What habits might need replacing with something healthier?

Chapter 3

Good Riddance
(Time of Your Life)

Good Riddance (Time of Your Life)
by Green Day – from their album **Nimrod**

I got Nimrod on a trip to America in 1998 and this album is the one that helped me through my parents' divorce.

When I was 14, I landed my first job in a hotel as a chambermaid in one of the nicer hotels in the area. However, after disposing of used condoms from the floor and cleaning pubic hair out of a bath, I began to question where my life was going!

It seemed that the universe knew chambermaiding wasn't for me, because I got sacked – for something I didn't do. They accused me of sleeping on a bed, which I hadn't. My dad took the call and politely brushed it off. I would probably have defended myself if they'd spoken to me, but in truth, I hated the job, so I wasn't that bothered to lose it.

After that, I worked at WHSmith in Andover, selling pens on the pen counter. It sounds niche but I really loved that job, and I was good at it. I even won a 100% mystery shopper award for amazing customer service.

This was where my love of rewards came from, and I think where I started to become a people pleaser. I loved it when people told me I was doing a good job. So, I was a bloody good employee. The more I did well, the more praise I got, and that became a cycle.

I loved shopping – and now I was earning my own money to spend. During my lunch break, I would wander around the shops and that wander would always include a visit to Marks & Spencer (M&S). I wouldn't ever make myself lunch because I was totally obsessed with the M&S ham, cheese and pickle sandwiches. I'd have the same sandwich every single day and I never questioned why! I would obsessively think about this sandwich, and if there was ever a time it wasn't there, I would cry – like a baby. You might not have obsessed over M&S ham, cheese and pickle sandwiches, but I'm sure you can relate.

This kind of hyperfixation on a specific type of food is common among those of us with ADHD. There have been numerous times in my life when I'd eat the same thing over and over, sometimes until it literally made me sick or I hit a point where I had eaten so much of it that I never wanted it again.

I'm sure you know that feeling where you know you should expand your horizons but you just can't bring yourself to do it. Then one day, all of a sudden, you'll change your take-away order or pick a differ-ent sandwich.

Whenever I didn't have work, I would shop. I loved everything about going shopping – the bus ride in, being with my friends and, of course, the actual shop-ping. Buying things made me happy. I started by shop-ping for little things, like lip balm, or sweets. Then I saved for bigger things, like trainers and clothes. My money never lasted long. If I wasn't buying physical items, I was spending my money on gig tickets and anything else music related.

CDs were my nemesis – I just couldn't resist buying them. I had a collection of thousands. I particularly loved rock, punk and metal music when I was 15 (to be fair, I still do) and one of my favourite ways to spend time at the weekend was to go to record fairs with my dad, where I could buy more CDs.

Music was my hyperfocus. When we were doing work experience through school and I got a placement at a record shop, I was ecstatic, even though I don't think my parents were too happy. Working in the record shop brought me so much joy. Music was my big love, and I knew so much about it already that talking to people about it was easy. I felt quite smug that while all my friends were working in law firms or offices, I was talking about music.

I was 15 and my spending addiction had already started, I just wasn't aware of it. I got money, I spent it. I made some more, I spent it. I never saved.

I left WHSmith and went to work on the checkouts at Iceland, the supermarket chain. I found sitting at the till all day painful, but I would amuse myself by looking at the cheap food people were buying. I loved it when someone found a reduced item – sometimes you could pick up products for as little as 10p. I used to get dopamine from others finding discounts.

But I used to get my own dopamine hit by finding discounted items for myself. One of the perks of the job was that you could wander around the shop in search of discounted items. I would fill up a trolley with bargains – think reduced prawn crackers, yum yums and other naughty food – and keep it in the back of the store so I could buy it at the end of my shift. Plus, I could apply my staff discount to what I bought, making them even bigger bargains.

Of course, I also got a dopamine kick from eating the food I bought – double whammy. I loved food, a bit too much.

FIRST LOVE

Around this time, I met Trevor (name changed – as if I would actually go out with a Trevor! P.S.: Sorry if your name is Trevor!), who quickly became my boy-friend. He was in a band, and he had a shaved head with green spikes at the front and an eyebrow pierc-ing. He was so cool. We would talk about music for hours.

He became my world. I was in love, and I didn't feel alone any more. This wasn't the kind of limerence love I'd experienced with Gary. This was real first-time love. I found sex, which meant my shopping stopped for a bit. Sex was way more fun, and I got addicted to the dopamine it gave me pretty quickly.

It took my mind off the stuff that was going down at school. I was still the blabbermouth, and I still didn't have many friends, but Trevor made me feel like noth-ing else mattered. When I had him, I didn't need any-one else. Again, another example of my people hyperfocus.

CRAMMING AND EXAMS

I started my exams. I really struggled to revise – which I'm sure you can also relate to. I would cram on the bus on the way to school hoping it would stick. But I would get into the exam room and my mind would be blank. I felt like every word I wrote was hard. My hand hurt, even holding a pen was hard.

What I've learnt since then is that those of us with ADHD experience task paralysis, which means, unless there is an urgent time pressure, we don't do things that often seem to come naturally to those who are neurotypical. That's why I'd often be the person doing my homework on the bus into school or in the playground. I'd always leave it to the last minute. Or, typically, the dog ate it!

With exams, there's the added challenge of our working memory. It doesn't matter how much you revise if your working memory can't recall the information when you're in an exam. When you're staring at a blank piece of paper and nothing comes to you, you're screwed. I found my exams really stressful, and I struggled. It's not that I'm unintelligent; it's simply that this mode of testing knowledge doesn't work for me – or the vast majority of other people with ADHD.

I remember getting so stressed about one exam that I broke out in hives all over my body. I just knew that I wasn't going to do well. I started blaming myself. Why had I messed about so much? Why didn't I do the work? Maybe if I hadn't been so obsessed with Trevor my grades would have been better.

But what I now know is that it wasn't my fault at all. In fact, I didn't do too badly, all things considered. I got an A* in French, because I loved learning languages and it came naturally to me. I also got two As in English, and the rest of my grades were mostly Bs and Cs, with a D in history – not too shabby.

When I look back on my time at school, I can see that if I didn't like the teacher of a specific subject, I would switch off. I've also been diagnosed with dyscalculia as an adult, which explains why I found subjects like maths and science so hard. But I also know that I get dopamine from learning something new, which is why I make sure that everyone on my courses learns by doing so that the information actually sticks.

And, in the midst of my exams, my parents were getting divorced, which certainly didn't help with my focus.

TURNING MY WORLD UPSIDE DOWN

My parents' divorce was really hard for me. I thought they would be together forever. I wondered if I had done something to make them separate. I questioned whether, maybe, if I had been a better daughter and if I didn't fight with my sister so much, things might have been different.

In truth, I ignored a lot of what was happening at home because I didn't know how to deal with it. I stuck my head in the sand. I spent time at Trevor's house, or at my friends' houses, instead of being at home. I did my own thing. As I now know, ignoring a problem is very typical for those of us with ADHD – we just hope it'll go away if we don't think about it. Of course, it doesn't.

Ignoring my parents' divorce was the worst thing I could have done for myself. I didn't even say goodbye to our family home when we sold it because I was so intent on ignoring what was happening around me. That caused trauma, which wasn't my parents' fault, but it affected me deeply.

My dad was my hero, and all of a sudden he wasn't around anymore. This triggered my rejection sensitivity dysphoria and I felt like it was all my fault. Of course, as an adult I understand that relationships break up for all kinds of reasons, and that it is highly unlikely to be because of a child's behaviour. But at the time, all I saw was two people I loved separating, and I couldn't understand it on that level.

If you've had an experience of divorce, then you'll know some of the many reasons that can lead to a relationship breaking down. Every divorce will have its unique set of circumstances, but if you are a child or teenager, it's difficult to understand all of the nuances of these kinds of relationships. All I can say to you if you experienced something similar is that it almost certainly wasn't your fault, but I know this won't have stopped the feelings of guilt, responsibility and sheer confusion that your parents divorcing introduces to your life.

The irony is that, although those of us with ADHD thrive in chaos, we need a structure to be able to navigate our day-to-day lives. We don't like change, but when your parents get divorced, all the routines you've relied on your whole life get turned upside down. Especially if you have autism too.

Suddenly you're at your mum's one weekend and your dad's the next. It is such a big change to your norm that it can put huge pressure on you. My advice in this kind of situation is to find a therapist, ideally one who is an ADHD specialist.

I'm a big believer in therapy and coaching for those of us who are neurodivergent because it helps us have healthier relationships with friends, family and partners by giving us someone we can talk openly to about the challenges we face.

Finding Support

Check out the *Mad About Money* app to find a list of therapists and coaches who have specific knowledge of ADHD and other neurodivergent conditions; its free in the app stores.

Gems of Wisdom

- Learn what you enjoy and try to find a job that plays to your strengths because you'll perform much better when you do.

- Be aware of your tendency to hyperfocus on specific things and people. Can you recognise when you find a new hyperfocus?

- Pretending your problems aren't there isn't a solution. It's only by facing up to them that you'll be able to solve them and lead a happier life.

Chapter 4

Butterfly

> **Butterfly by Crazy Town – *from their album*
> The Gift of Game**
>
> This song was released when I was at college,
> Everything I did was a bit more flamboyant,
> and I turned into a social butterfly.

I started college. Freedom! It felt amazing to be going
to college and hanging out with my friends every day
in the refectory. I went to my lectures – the ones I
liked! I chose Art, Fashion, Media and English, but in
honesty I was way more interested in college for the
social life than my courses.

I was voted in as President of the Student's Union,
which made me super popular, because I could give

people the wrong date of birth on their student ID. I know this was super illegal, and all I can say is that my intentions weren't to break the law I just wanted everyone to be included.

The way I saw it back then, making someone a year older than they really were just meant that we could all hang out in the same places. I wanted everyone to have the same access as each other, and I wanted everyone to feel like they were part of the crowd. I was impulsive and I shouldn't have done it, but I didn't think about the consequences.

I charged £10 to change someone's date of birth on their ID. All of this earned me popularity and money. But, of course, I wasn't sophisticated – I just had a Tippex pen and a laminator! Within a year, I had been found out and that venture ended. But it did show me that I had the creativity to find other ways of making money that didn't involve working for someone else. You could say this was an early sign of my entrepreneurial spirit.

Six months into my college journey Trevor dumped me. It felt like someone had died. I had never lost anyone before. I felt sick. I had lost my best friend, and my person. He was my rock through my parents' divorce and my fallouts with friends. I really loved him.

I was absolutely devastated, especially as he dumped me for someone who looked almost identical to me and who was likely more neurotypical. I think the worst part was that he cheated on me with her. He even once joked on the phone about having an affair with someone from his university, which, as it turned out, wasn't a joke.

We'd been together for two-and-a-half years, and he'd been so kind to me. But it wasn't just Trevor who I lost during our breakup. I liked his friends, who were a little alternative and who I felt just 'got' me more than my friends did. His parents were also really kind to me, especially as I spent so much time at his house when my parents were divorcing.

I missed his family. I missed the things we did together. He distracted me, in a good way, during a rocky period of my life. While I was with Trevor, we had moved house. My mum had a new boyfriend who she had moved in with, and we had moved to a new village called West Wellow. They were building an extension on the house, which meant I didn't have a bedroom, so I had my own caravan in the garden. I even had a new family; Chris, my mum's boyfriend, had two kids who were young adults, and we all got on pretty well.

Trevor had been with me through all those ups and downs. He was the first person I had sex with and, I think like many of us at that age, I naively thought he was the person I'd spend the rest of my life with. It's true that we had a lot in common, but we also had some awful fights, in part because I struggled to regulate my emotions.

Tips for Dealing with a Breakup When You Have ADHD

- Allow yourself to grieve, notice your emotions and don't feel bad for having them.

- Put as much space between you and the other person as possible to allow you to move on.

- Don't keep anything around that reminds you of them; it only makes it worse.

- Don't be tempted to have revenge sex, especially with their best friend. Trust me, it doesn't feel good afterwards.

- Get therapy and talk to a professional who understands.

- Create healthy habits and practices in your life. Don't get really pissed or spend your salary online shopping – that won't make the pain go away.

- Get your dopamine hits from friends, exercise and music.

- Cry it out! Let the tears go – it's cathartic and it helps.

- I've always found it helps to think that everything happens for a reason, but the first time your heart gets broken is the worst because it feels like the pain will never end. Trust me when I say that it will. You'll never forget your first love, but you will move on and be happy again.

- Remember that your RSD will intensify your feelings when you get dumped.

Mine and Trevor's breakup was really hard on me. You never forget your first love, whether you're neurotypical or neurodivergent, but the grief I felt over the end of our relationship was intense and it lasted for months. It was particularly hard to go to events with all of our friends and see him with his new girlfriend, who looked just like me, but who was a bit quieter and a little older. Of course, that triggered my RSD.

With Trevor no longer in my life, I also had to face up to the fact that my parents had got divorced. Also, we'd moved to a new house, and I now lived in a caravan in our front garden.

ADJUSTING TO A NEW WAY OF LIFE

Although I struggled with a lot of the changes happening in my life at this time, living in the caravan was great. It was like moving out and having my own space without having to pay any bills or rent.

But it was hard adjusting to my life without my dad there. I really missed him, and as a result I was a bit of a brat to Chris, my mum's new boyfriend, for the first year we lived with him, which he didn't deserve. He was the best thing to ever happen to my mum (and us, for that matter). He was loving, caring and supportive, and he took her and her two kids in. I was a stroppy, ungrateful teenager.

Twenty-five years on, I love him like a dad. He has done so much for me personally, and I'm forever regretful of being such a douche to him when we first moved in. Chris also brought his children, Emily and Matt, into our family, and they're awesome. Even though Emily and I had nothing in common as teenagers, we became very close and we're still close to this day.

Around the time I moved into the caravan, I started working in the local pub as a barmaid. It really wasn't my scene, but I got lots of tips. Most of the people my age thought I was weird. I couldn't find any common ground with them. I had bright hair, piercings and I dressed like I should have been in the Sex Pistols, so I was just a bit 'odd'.

But my time at college was when I committed to being myself – no matter what. I drove to college every day. I hung out in Andover most weekends and stayed at friends' houses. I got my first tattoo – a little rainbow on my bum. I didn't tell my mum because I knew she would hit the roof!

This was also when I found a friend who was just as quirky as me, Kiki. We liked all the same bands, so we started going to gigs and hanging out backstage. She did the merch for a band called Spunge, and we used to hang out with them. We went to lots of festivals and gigs, and there were lots of things to spend my very little money on.

I decided I wanted to go to university when I finished college. It was the expected thing to do back then.

I didn't go on a gap year, which is one thing I will always regret. All I wanted was to go away and start living my life. I worked all summer at the pub, and I also worked at the jewellery shop Claire's Accessories in Southampton, which I loved.

By the time the summer was over, I had saved up around £1,000 to go to university with, only because I had my mum checking on me. We put 25% of my allowance away every month, and I used to transfer some of my wages each week for my mum to put in the same account that I couldn't access, because I knew I spent whatever I earned otherwise.

To be honest, it wouldn't have mattered how much I'd saved. I didn't know how to budget or manage my money, so it was always going to be an utter disaster. Before I went to university, I never had any experience of paying bills or budgeting, which I think is essential.

For anyone who is reading this who has teens – talk to them and make sure that they understand money before they leave home. It would have saved me so many problems. I should probably add here that my mum tried to teach me, but I just wasn't interested. Had I been interested, it could have made the next 10 years of my life a lot more bearable. Had I known I had ADHD, things could also have been so different.

Gems of Wisdom

- Dealing with a breakup when you have ADHD is intense. Let yourself grieve and feel your emotions. It feels like the pain will never end, but I promise it does.

- Explore creative (but legal) ways to make extra money. If you have an idea for a business, test the waters and see how it goes.

- If you know you struggle to save money, get some help. Ask a parent or someone else you really trust to hold you accountable for saving, like my mum did, or set up an account that you pay into each month but that you can't access easily.

Chapter 5

Don't Let Me Get Me

Don't Let Me Get Me *by P!nk – from her album* **Missundaztood**

'I'm a hazard to myself'. This song represents the beginning of my self-destruction. It's a reminder that I'm my own worst enemy and also that the only person who can help me is me.

I went to university in Leicester DMU , which I picked based on the nightlife – the city has three rock clubs – as well as Demon FM, the student radio station. It had won awards and was the best student radio station in the country. I didn't want a proper job. All I ever wanted was to be a radio presenter.

After ticking off the rock clubs and radio station boxes, I needed a media studies course. Little did I know I was again chasing dopamine. Hunting dopamine is a theme that runs throughout my life. As you'll hear later in the book, there were situations that made me realise I needed to change my life, but at the time I didn't understand **why** I needed to change and I also didn't realise that when I made changes, I was just shifting my dopamine hunting from one thing to another. None of this truly became clear to me until I received my ADHD diagnosis.

But back to my younger self who was just starting university and whose only goals were being a radio presenter and being famous, I had always idolised TV presenter Davina McCall, since her **Streetmate** and **Big Brother** days. I loved everything about her. She had such incredible energy and the way she interviewed random people on the street **Streetmate** reminded me of how I was – I used to do that all the time, I just didn't have a camera crew following me around! I thought I needed to study media studies if I wanted to get into radio and TV like her.

I wish I had actually paid attention in my lectures, because it was a great course. I learned video editing, PR, marketing, TV studies – all of which are skills I now use as a *TikTok* influencer! But I mostly found the lectures boring and despite my passion for being on the radio, I struggled to motivate myself. I was hungover most of the time, and at this stage of my life, I found the practical nature of the lectures boring. TV editing, filming angles and composition weren't my passion – radio was. Ultimately, it wasn't the course for me.

I spent time at the radio station every day, where I was creating slots and segments and actually presenting on the radio which I loved. Looking back now, I can see how the structure of the lectures just wasn't compatible with my ADHD.

What's really interesting is that almost 20% of UK-domiciled undergraduate students in the 2023–2024 academic year are neurodivergent or have a disability.[1] In 2022–2023, there were just over two million undergraduate students enrolled in UK universities, which equates to around 400,000 neurodivergent students at the undergraduate level alone.[2]

---

[1] Marks, H. (no date) *What is neurodiversity?* https://www.plymouth.ac.uk/discover/what-is-neurodiversity
[2] HESA, (Aug 2024) *Figure 3 – HE student enrollments by level of study 2018/19 to 2022/23.* https://www.hesa.ac.uk/data-and-analysis/sb269/figure-3

Those statistics don't surprise me, because those of us who are neurodivergent are more likely to follow our passion than anyone else. We have a thirst for knowledge, and we will dedicate ourselves to one thing, or hyperfocus on one thing, that captures our interest. And it's likely there are so many more people who think they are neurodivergent or just don't know yet.

When I was at university, awareness of neurodivergent conditions was a lot lower than it is now, but even so, I was still given a laptop to help me with my dyslexia, and a support grant of £500 that was supposed to be for additional resources. If I'm honest, I probably spent it getting drunk.

Getting Support in an Education Setting

- **Take breaks:** move your body to stay focused.

- **Ask for support:** extensions and exam accommodations are more accessible than ever.

- **Stay engaged in lectures:** try doodling, crocheting, or even closing your eyes to focus.

- **Disclose if you're comfortable:** tutors may offer support you didn't know existed.

The one good thing about my course was that I met Zoe, who became one of my best friends. I met her on day one, while we were queuing to choose our modules (yep, nothing online back then!). She is a beautiful, slightly quirky Welsh girl with a similar sense of alternative style to me. I started talking to her. 'Hiya babe!!!', her Welsh accent grated on me, and I vowed never to speak to her again. But the universe had other plans.

Zoe ended up being in almost all of my lectures and we quickly became lunch buddies – it didn't take me long to realise I'd misjudged her. She would body-double me to help me go to lectures, and when I missed one, she would let me borrow her notes. Often, she'd drop me a message on MSN Messenger to tell me what I'd missed. She was, and still is, really kind and one of my favourite people on this planet.

We had so much fun together and we never stopped being friends. I felt like she understood me more than anyone else and she still does to this day. Nearly 22 years later, she is still my best friend, and I couldn't imagine life without her!

Of course, I also met all of my housemates on my first day of uni. None of them seemed to have anything in common with me, which was fine, although it did make me uncomfortable. When I'm uncomfortable, I drink more booze. I wanted to try and fit in, so I got pretty pissed on Lambrini mixed with summer fruit squash – it was cheap, that's all I'll say!

THE START OF A VERY SLIPPERY SLOPE

The next day I went to the Freshers' Fair. I was totally hanging and ready to pick up some freebies. I managed to get mugs, pens and shopping bags. But most notably I managed to find trouble.

As I walked into the Freshers' Fair, I was met by loads of banks and credit card providers. I was not expecting them to be offering sign up bonuses, like gift cards, vouchers and overdrafts. I signed up with three different banks for six credit cards, just for the freebies. They were offering things like pizza, vouchers and 'free' cash! As I signed up for all of them, I told myself I wouldn't use them. How wrong I was! This was definitely the point where it all started to go very wrong.

Resisting Temptation

If you find yourself in a similar situation, either at university or at any other stage in your life, ask yourself the following questions **before** you sign on the dotted line:

- Do you need a credit card?

- Is debt something you need in your life? (Probably not!)

- Could you get a job? I had a job at this stage, but what I didn't have was a budget, so I didn't realise that I was overspending, let alone by how much.

- Be disciplined and remind yourself of what you really need. Use the mantra: **Pause. Breathe. What's the need?**

I was living the party lifestyle and spending money like it was going out of print. I prioritised the dopamine hit of going out, drinking, dancing, listening to music and talking to boys. At the beginning, my extra spending wasn't too out of control. I'd buy the odd take away or outfit. But the more I spent the better I would feel, and spending money became a new obsession.

At no point did I track how much I was spending – if I had, then I might have realised how much I was overspending.

Think You're Overspending?

- Start tracking your spending. It might feel scary, but it's much better to know where you stand.

- Ask yourself if what you're spending your money on is adding value to your life. A good question is: Is this pushing me forward or am I just buying this for the dopamine?

- Think about why you're spending money – is it because you're depressed? Or because you're bored? Or to fill time? Or even happy spending.

- When you better understand **why** you're spending money, ask yourself: What else can I do that gives me dopamine but that doesn't involve spending money? Could you go to the gym, go for a walk, have a bath or even read a book?

After the Christmas break, all my housemates at university decided they hated me and to this day I'm still not sure why we fell out. My most educated guess is that I was super annoying! Living in halls became a total nightmare. I was scared to go to the toilet in case I saw people and I was going out every night just to avoid being there. I started spending more.

I would buy clothes, shoes and bags. I wanted to feel like I was fitting into a world where I felt totally alone. But I would get buyer's remorse, instantly feeling guilty about spending money I knew wasn't mine to spend. On one level, I knew I would have to pay it back at some point, but on another, it felt like free money. I continually felt bad about buying things. Sometimes they wouldn't even fit me, but I couldn't be bothered to take things back, which made me feel worse and then I spent more to cheer myself up. It was a vicious cycle.

Research from Tesco Bank in 2024 found that almost half (48%) of 18–24 year olds are in debt. This rises to 65% of 25–30 year olds. Scarily, credit cards are the main form of borrowing among those in the younger age group. Those aged 18–24 are also more likely to owe family members money, be overdrawn and to have used buy now, pay later schemes than other UK adults.[3]

So, if any of this sounds familiar, you really aren't alone – even though I know it can feel that way.

---

[3] Tesco Bank, *Three fifths of UK adults think children need to be aware of debt before 18th birthday* (6 March 2024). https://bank.tescoplc.com/three-fifths-of-uk-adults-think-children-need-to-be-aware-of-debt-before-18th-birthday/

Drinking really didn't help. The more I boozed, which was pretty much every night, the worse I felt the next day, and the more money I spent. I was in a vicious cycle of spending, drinking and sleeping around. I got a reputation for being 'slutty', and what I didn't realise at the time was that this was just another form of dopamine hunting for me.

I needed love and I was searching for someone who wanted me as much as I wanted them. I was impulsive but then I'd feel incredibly rejected if I slept with someone who later ignored me.

This pattern of behaviour went on for four years! I didn't think about it until much later in my life, but I now realise I was going through trauma. I was feeling abandoned by my ex-boyfriend and by my parents getting divorced.

A GROWING SPENDING PROBLEM

I ran out of room in my wardrobe because I bought new clothes every day, so they went on the floor. Nothing had a place. I hated the mess, but I couldn't bring myself to tidy it. I moved my room around all the time to try and avoid the mess, which later I found out was very much an ADHD thing to do.

By this point, I had moved into a house on Winchester Avenue with some friends I met at a rock club in Leicester. I already had problems with money when I moved in here – way more problems than I was admitting to myself. I had maxed out all my credit cards, and I was in blissful denial about how many people I owed money to.

I started to fall behind on my rent payments and my share of the bills, which made my house mates really cross with me. They would ask me when I was paying, I would always say 'when I can' even though I knew full well I didn't have the money and had no idea where it was coming from.

I went out every night to avoid awkward conversations, but I also drank so much I put myself into dangerous situations. This made my housemates even more angry, because they couldn't understand how I could afford to go out when I couldn't afford to pay my bills. The answer was simple, I couldn't put my rent on a credit card, but booze and shopping were a different story! Plus, booze and partying gave me dopamine, paying bills didn't.

I was desperate for help, but I had nowhere to turn. I couldn't tell my parents; I knew they would be ashamed of me. Every time my mum called me, I would tell her I was off to a lecture, or I was in the middle of something. I felt terrible not talking to her. But as an oversharer, I knew if I talked to her, I would end up telling her how much debt I was in. I didn't want to burden her. I was very much a people pleaser, and I didn't want to let her down.

I wish I had told her sooner. It would have saved so much heartache, and the guilt and shame would have been short lived. I was a mess mentally and physically.

I recognised that I was in trouble, and I heard about some support the university offered, so I asked for some help. The woman I spoke to looked me up and down as though she thought I was the scum of the earth with my bright pink and turquoise hair, ripped jeans, pink Rancid t-shirt and piercings all over the place.

I sat down and cried. I told her I couldn't pay my rent, and that I'd maxed out my credit cards. This was the first time I had openly told anyone that I was struggling. And it was hard. I felt so judged and ashamed of my situation. I got a hardship loan of £1,500 and a hardship grant of £500 from the university, which in hindsight didn't really help me; I was in a spiral and I couldn't fix it. As soon as that was gone, I was still in trouble with my credit cards.

What they should have done was help me to budget. Looking back, I can see that if I had known how to budget from the start, I wouldn't have been in this mess – or at the very least I wouldn't have been in so much of a mess. But my undiagnosed ADHD made me impulsive, and I was doing everything I could to fit in. Drinking made my brain numb. It gave me confidence, and it helped me to feel normal. Of course, it also cost money.

How to Start a Budget

There are some simple things you can do to start getting to grips with budgeting. Whether you think you're overspending or not, I recommend that you do this exercise because it has the power to set you up for life.

1. Write down everything you buy for two weeks.

2. Categorise each purchase – is it something essential, like rent or a bill payment, or is it something fun?

3. Look at each item and ask yourself, 'Do I need this in my life? Does this support my life?'

4. Compare how much you're spending with how much you're bringing in. If the two align, or you're spending less than you're earning, you may not need to cut back. If you're spending more than you're earning, use your categorised expenses to help you work out where to cut back.

Categorise literally everything! The more you can give every penny or pound you spend a purpose in your life, the easier it is to save and to invest. Having a budget also gives you confidence that every last thing in your life is paid for – trust me that's a great feeling!

WHAT TO PUT IN YOUR BUDGET

The following are the main things to consider included in your budget for each week or month:

- Essential bills
  - Mortgage/rent
  - Utilities (gas, electric, water)
  - Home repairs
- A personal care and lifestyle expenses
  - Groceries
  - Subscriptions (Netflix, TV licence, phone, broadband, Amazon Prime, etc.)
  - Makeup
  - Clothing and shoes
  - Self-care
  - Socialising
  - Hobbies
  - Medication
- Transport
  - Car payments
  - Insurance
  - Tax/MOT/maintenance
  - Petrol/gas
  - Bus/train fares

- Pet care
  - Vet bills
  - Pet food
  - Insurance
- Children
  - Childcare
  - After school clubs
  - Holiday clubs
  - Hobbies
  - Pocket money
  - Toys/books
  - Birthday parties
- Holidays and gifting
  - Birthday presents
  - Christmas
  - Easter eggs (if applicable)
  - Saving for vacations
- Fun
  - Concerts
  - Festivals
  - Events
- Saving and debts
  - 'What if' fund (this sounds nicer than 'emergency fund')
  - Debt repayments

Instead of having a 'what if fund', I have a 'rainbow fund', which I can use for anything I need. Personally, I avoid using the term 'emergency fund' because I don't want to manifest emergencies in my life. My rule with my 'rainbow fund' is that it has to be a little difficult to access, so that I can't just dip into it for frivolous items, but having that money available gives me security to know that I can manage unexpected expenses. My 'rainbow fund' sits in **Plum**, which is a financial app designed to help you save.

Spread the Cost

There will be certain expenses that crop up every year, like the MOT for your car, renewing any insurance you pay for annually, even Christmas shopping. Factor those into your monthly budget too.

It's much easier to save £8 a month towards your MOT than to suddenly have to find £100 when you realise it's due.

The truth is that you don't know where you need to cut back until you have a budget, so creating one has to be your starting point. This isn't always an exercise in limiting your spending, and it's certainly not about cutting out all the fun things in your life.

This is about making sure you are enjoying your life and that you're not storing up debt issues with your spending. I will never tell someone to stop buying something they enjoy – if you love buying your daily coffee, go for it.

It's your life, so put the things that you want to budget for in your world on that list. If it turns out you don't have enough money for that thing, the next step is to work out how you can make some extra money or maybe where you can save some money to cover it.

Have a Money Date Each Month

Set a date each month when you have a money date with yourself to review your budget and your overall finances. Get a glass of wine or a cup of tea, make something nice to eat and set aside a couple of hours to go through your bank account, check that against your budget and make sure everything lines up. Make sure that you have covered everything on the list I just shared.

The key to doing this regularly is to make it a pleasant experience, so give yourself whatever treat you need to motivate you. You might find it works better to give yourself a treat after you've been through your budget and finances. Do whatever works for you.

CHANGE YOUR MINDSET

If you keep thinking that you're rubbish with money, guess what? You'll keep being rubbish with money. This applies in any area of life. If you think you'll be bad at something, you will be.

So, if you keep telling yourself things like the following, you are in a mindset of lack:

- I don't have enough money for this.

- I'm too poor for that.

- I waste money.

- I never have enough.

- Money is hard to earn.

Any of those sound familiar? When you're in a lack mindset, everything in your life will reflect that. It will show up in the quality of your life, in your finances and in your living situation.

What you need to do is flip your way of thinking and develop an abundance mindset. Start telling yourself things like:

- I'm learning to make more money.

- I have more money.

- Money flows easily to me.

- Every day I make more money.

When you make these abundance-focused phrases part of your internal monologue, those things start happening and I am a testament to this. Flip the script*, change your thought process and start telling yourself positive affirmations about money. You'll be amazed at the changes you see in your life.

Focus on one big goal: ADHD brains get distracted, so keep it front of mind.

Believe it's possible: start with something exciting but realistic to keep your motivation strong.

Find relatable role models: seeing others like you succeed strengthens belief.

Write it down: keep your goal visible, use a vision board if needed.

Set daily intentions: state what you want to achieve and how you want to feel.

Visualisation helps, but isn't essential: if you can, do it morning and night.

Use your imagination: if manifesting a home, visit houses and picture yourself living there.

Since I discovered the power of manifestation, my life has changed significantly and it's my passion to teach and share its virtues and help others change their lives.

Also accept that this way of thinking has often been ingrained in us from a young age. We're told we have to work hard so we can earn money, but the truth is that it's about working smarter, not harder. It's about setting goals, giving your spending and your saving a specific purpose, and being grateful for what you have.

HEAD IN THE SAND

I started to get debt collectors' letters. I didn't know what to do with them. They were coming in thick and fast. Every time I got a letter, I would be terrified. I hid bills under the doormat, and it got so bad that I would trip over it when I entered the house. I would ignore phone calls and keep on avoiding my housemates, so I didn't have to admit that I had massively fluffed up*. Anytime an unknown number called, I would hide my phone.

I felt like I was a criminal. I felt like I had done something awful. The people at the university who I spoke to about hardship support had been so judgy, I didn't know what to do. My mental health had never been worse. I was drinking more and more.

WHEN DOPAMINE GOES WRONG

Trigger warning: the following section contains details of sexual assault, rape and suicidal thoughts.

One night I was out for one of my housemates' birthdays. I got really drunk which was a standard thing for me to do. But that night my drink was spiked while I was in the club. This resulted in a traumatic sexual assault.

We went back to our house for a house party, where I was raped by three people in my bedroom. I don't have full memories of the night – only flashes. I knew one of the men involved, but not the other two. It was horrific; I was completely violated. I went to the police, who couldn't do anything because although they could prove that the incident had occurred, they said there was no evidence of a lack of consent.

You have to remember, this was 20 years ago, long before the #MeToo movement. Because I'd been drinking, and because I was promiscuous, there was very much a sense that I could have consented, even though I know that I didn't. Even my housemates didn't really believe me – looking back I can understand why, but it made me feel totally alone. No one would support me or back me up.

After that incident I became a recluse. I stayed in my room and cried. I felt dirty, used and horrible. I didn't want to leave the house. I stopped going to the radio station, and I considered taking my own life. Nobody wanted me there. I had never felt so alone.

I stopped going out as much, which should have been better for my bank account, but I was spending more than I ever had to try and numb the pain.

I drank more, just at home, and I ate a lot of unhealthy food. I was buying takeaways almost every night because I didn't have the drive to do anything else. I lost the will to live and felt as though my soul and purpose had been sucked out of me.

Shopping was the only thing that made me feel good; it would take me away from overthinking and the dark thoughts in my mind. This was long before the days of the internet – Jesus what would I have been like if I'd had online shopping? I enjoyed the experience of shopping, from the part where I would walk around the shops, to physically handing over my cards to buy an item. But as soon as I got home the guilt would set in, making me feel so much worse.

I felt ashamed, but I found the courage to tell my mum that I'd been raped. She was obviously worried about me, but she didn't know how to help. She wanted me to come home, which I did for a bit when I came down with glandular fever, no doubt because I was so stressed. This gave me post-viral fatigue syndrome, which completely zapped my energy levels. All I wanted to do was sleep.

My housemates thought I was lazy because I'd sleep, get up and go out for my dopamine hit and then go back to bed. I stopped going to my lectures and I backed away from the radio station. I only did the things I really had to. At this point in my life, money facilitated all of my dopamine hits.

ADDICTED TO SPENDING

I was addicted to spending money. But I didn't realise it. I was also addicted to drinking. Both things were making me happy then sad. A spending addiction is actually really serious, and people don't talk about it enough.

What makes a spending addiction harder is that you can't just stop shopping like you can drinking. You will always have to spend money, even if it's just on the bare essentials. That means you need to learn how to regulate your spending because you can't just quit spending cold turkey as an adult.

Of course, if you don't know you have a problem, then it makes it almost impossible to actually do anything about it.

Once you recognise you have a spending addiction, try to recognise the emotion behind your spending. Are you sad? Bored? Happy even? When you can put an emotion to the spending, you're starting to dig into the root cause of the problem. Nine times out of ten, the emotion you're feeling when you spend will be your trigger.

It's also important to note that the emotion that triggers you might not be negative – it's not uncommon for people to spend when they're happy. I know that when I'm happy and feel like I have something to celebrate that I'll treat myself to a new outfit, go out drinking or find something else to spend my money on.

This is all about developing your awareness around why you spend, so that you can spend in a more mindful way. For instance, while I was writing this book,

I had my best month ever in my business. I told myself that I could have a reward – I had my eye on a Kurt Geiger handbag. But instead of buying it from Kurt Geiger, I found it on Vinted where it cost me a fraction of the full price.

Tips for Dealing with ADHD Impulse Spending

- Don't beat yourself up. It's hard enough dealing with the shame of spending too much without the added pressure of hating yourself for it.

- Try to put barriers in between you and spending. Work out where you spend the most. It seems obvious, but try not to go to those places. If it's Amazon or Deliveroo, remove those apps from your phone, or disconnect your card so you have to manually type in your card number at the checkout.

- Set yourself some rules. Make it into a game – give yourself points and rewards for not spending. Set challenges to save some money when you feel like spending, that can also give you dopamine.

- Don't restrict your spending too much, if it's like a diet you will get bored and you will crack. Give yourself a treat occasionally.

- Try to remove yourself from situations where you are more likely to spend on things you don't

(continued)

need. For example, I either shop online or send my husband so that I don't get distracted by shiny things.

- Make a list of all of the things you buy, recognise the emotion, but also recognise if it's a need or a want. Wants are good but within reason.

- Unsubscribe from shopping emails. They are just prompting you to spend money on things you don't always need.

Breaking a spending addiction is really tough, but I've found it helpful to have a list of things I can do that don't involve spending money. Whenever I feel like I want to spend, I can go to my list and choose a free activity instead. Here are five to get you started:

1. **Get creative:** Drawing, doodling and painting are all great ways to take your mind off spending. Just use whatever paper and pens/pencils/paint you have to hand.

2. **Exercise:** Go for a run, find a free workout video on YouTube or a free yoga practice. Moving your body is free.

3. **Listen to a podcast:** There are thousands of fascinating podcasts available online, completely free of charge. Find a subject or person who interests you and learn something instead of spending money.

4. **Phone a friend:** Reach out to a friend or family member for a chat. Maybe even see if they're free to go for a walk too.

5. **Visit your local park:** Go for a walk in nature. It's free to sit in a park; you could even take a picnic or a book to read if you want.

For more ideas of things to do without spending money, check out the **Mad About Money** app.

USING CREDIT CARDS FOR GOOD

I know I've made credit cards sound like the devil, but they do have their advantages, provided that you can control your spending. Once I had cleared my debt, I used a credit card to help rebuild my credit rating. The rule is that you spend money on your credit card and clear it the same month. A top tip is to buy things you'd buy anyway – like groceries or fuel for your car – and then make sure you pay off the balance. But that's not the only way credit cards can be useful.

Consumer expert Helen Dewdney, who has the website www.thecomplainingcow.co.uk, shared the following insights and tips. She explains that you can use a credit card for purchases over £100 and under £30,000.

(continued)

- **CREDIT CARDS EXPLAINED** Under Section 75 of the Consumer Credit Act 1974, UK, the card issuer is jointly liable with the retailer for any purchases made, within certain limits. This is really great protection when you're booking a holiday.

- You need only pay 1p on the credit card, so long as the total transaction is more than £100.

- If a company falls into administration and you haven't received the purchase or service that you've paid for, you will be able to get the money refunded from the credit card company.

- The credit card company can also intervene if you have trouble getting a refund, repair or replacement from the trader, under consumer law.

- For purchases under £100 and for when using a debit card, the bank may operate the voluntary 'Chargeback' scheme, providing similar cover.

- If your card provider does not give you the appropriate redress, you can take the matter to the Financial Ombudsman Service at no cost.

- Set up a direct debit to pay off the full amount of your credit card bill every month.

- Alternatively, you can make the one-off payment as soon as you've paid on your credit card, so you do not need to worry about forgetting to pay.

Gems of Wisdom

- Don't be afraid to ask for support. When you're in debt it can feel very lonely, but there are people and organisations who can help.

- Make a budget. This is the best way to keep on top of your money and to identify where you're overspending.

- Dig into the emotions behind your spending. When you can see the root cause of overspending, it's much easier to spot your triggers and prevent yourself from making a purchase.

Chapter 6

I Just Wanna Live

I Just Wanna Live *by Good Charlotte – from their album* The Chronicles of Life and Death

This is a really empowering, fun song and it reminds me of putting my middle finger up to everyone and doing my own thing.

In 2005, I was beginning to feel more like myself, even though I still hadn't got to grips with my spending and my money. That's when I met Clive (again, name changed; as if!). He really 'got' me, and he understood what I had been through.

I had known of him for a while because we hung out in similar social circles. But it was only when I decided I was going to run for media officer working for the student's union that I started to get to know him properly. He was Scottish, suggestive with the eyes, and a bit of a ladies' man but could hold his own with the lads. He was tattooed, tall and skinny. In other words, not my usual rugby player type.

But we had lots in common, both music-wise and through our social circles. We were up against each other for the same position, and the banter and competition made me like him. I was desperate to find love. I didn't love myself at all, and that made me need someone else's love even more.

We campaigned for weeks outside the library trying to get votes. About half an hour before the results were announced, someone said, 'Maddy, can I have a word?' My brain immediately went into a negative spin. I instantly had sweaty palms and heart palpitations. 'Can I have a word?' is probably one of the worst things someone can say to you if you have ADHD.

'We have had to take you out of the running for media officer'.

'What? Why? What have I done?' I asked.

'You don't attend this university anymore Maddy!' My stomach hit the floor.

I had been so caught up in everything: the spending, the drinking, the assault. I hadn't realised that I hadn't been to any lectures for a really long time. I hadn't submitted my latest assignment and wasn't paying my fees, so I had been chucked off my course. Because I wasn't opening my post, I had missed the letters telling me I wasn't on my course anymore. I burst into tears.

This was the icing on the cake. I had spent three weeks campaigning for something I was passionate about, and I was now not able to do it. I was so cross with myself for not noticing how bad it had gotten. It was a wake-up call, although it wasn't my big wake-up call.

This was when I realised that I needed to grow up a bit. I had failed my university degree and all I had to show for my six years was a load of debt. I knew I wouldn't have any more student loan payments coming my way or any other student support. I was feeling really sorry for myself, but I was still burying my head in the sand when it came to the full extent of my money problems.

But this did act as a wake-up call that I didn't have to stay in Leicester. I didn't go to university anymore, so I could leave. After the assault, I felt like I was always looking over my shoulder in the city. Occasionally I'd even see the guys who had assaulted me, and who didn't seem to realise that what they'd done was wrong.

Clive was nearby when I heard the bombshell that I wasn't a student anymore. He took me to the pub. I wasn't really in a drinking mood, so we didn't stay long. The next thing I knew he was in my bed. He was very welcome there; it had been on the cards for a few weeks. I think it was safe to say we both quite liked each other.

That afternoon with Clive was the start of something new. I wasn't sure what we were, but I knew he saved me at that moment. Clive moved into my place quickly and we became inseparable. We didn't do much apart from bum around in my really skanky flat and watch boxsets. When I say skanky it was grim, it had black mould, it smelt like damp. I was constantly getting sick. But it was the cheapest place we could find – £270 a month!

We didn't do anything to make it more homely. I'm the kind of person who needs supervision to tidy or deal with any form of mess. Clive was not the kind of person to encourage me to tidy, or to do it himself. I don't remember ever using the kitchen in that flat – we used to order in or eat out. It was a mess.

Clive also wasn't in a great mental space. He'd recently come out of a relationship when we got together. We both needed comfort in some form, and we found that in sex, having a laugh and hiding away together.

After a few weeks, I knew I had to do something. I wasn't a student anymore which meant no more student loan payments. In truth I was quite thankful for that as my student loan was already quite high (around £26,000).

When I talk about my debts, I never actually factor in my student loan. If I did, at their worst, they would have been around £66,000! But the worst was yet to come. It hadn't sunk in just how bad my financial position was at that point.

Don't Ignore Your Debts...

- Debts only get worse the longer they're left unpaid. Interest is added and it's really easy for them to spiral.

- Your credit score will be impacted, which might affect your ability to get a mortgage or even a phone contract in the future. There's also a legal impact like debt collectors and county court judgements (CCJs).

- Your stress levels will go through the roof.

- Debt impacts those around you too – your friends, partner and family – especially if they live with you.

I started interviewing for jobs. At 24, I was technically an adult, but I didn't feel like one. I was still an 18 year old in my head.

I had no career aspirations; I just had to make money. So, I worked as a temp in the conference and banqueting team doing sales for Leicester Tigers Rugby club (which makes me a bit sick now as a Harlequins fan). I found it boring, and when something is boring, I have no motivation. Perhaps unsurprisingly, that job didn't last long.

I really wanted to work for a radio station, so I applied for Radio One and local radio, but there weren't many positions available. I had an interview for Leicester Sound to work in their advertising department, which would have been cool, but on the day of the interview I was hungover. I think they must have smelled the booze from the night before. I always seemed to sabotage myself.

All of this led me to a job working for a recruitment agency in town. It was the only thing I was offered, and I was desperate for money. I was responsible for calling up clients and arranging bookings. It wasn't proper recruitment, which I went on to do down the line. But it was a job.

For six months, I had money coming in. I wasn't bad at it either. But one day the managers came into the office and told us we were all being made redundant. I hadn't been there long enough to get any redundancy money!

> When you're in debt, it's best to pay something towards your debt, even if it's just a little bit, each month. This will stop people chasing you and mean you are making progress, even if it feels slow.

I had started to pay off some of the bills from my old house and my ex-housemates were not as cross with me, although I knew I had a lot of making up to do.

But losing my job made me feel like I was back to square one.

This was the last thing I needed. I was broken, and I wanted to give up. The bills were piling up, Clive had started to drink heavily, and we were basically penniless.

When you're at rock bottom, it feels like the world is conspiring against you. There have been several points in my life where all the bad stuff seems to happen at once – this was one of them. But I genuinely believe that when one thing after another goes wrong, you become low and it's almost as though you manifest more problems for yourself.

I know it's hard, but it's really important to find the positives in any situation and to be grateful for what you have.

Try to stop your negative self-talk in its tracks. Find one positive thing every day. If you can do that for three months, it will become a consistent habit. Consistency is key and three months is long enough for anything to become a habit.

WHAT CAN YOU DO WHEN THINGS GO WRONG?

It's quite common for ADHDers to catastrophise when things go wrong in our lives. One of the techniques I've found really helpful in moving past feeling

as though a setback is the end of the world is
to look back on other times in your life when
you've failed at something, or experienced something bad, and reminding yourself how you got
through it.

- Remind yourself that this feeling is temporary.

- Ask yourself what you can do that's positive.

- If you've lost money, flip your mindset. Instead of
  focusing on what you've lost, ask how you can make
  that money back.

Money in particular is very emotive. It makes the
world go round. When you don't have it, life can
feel incredibly difficult, but rather than focus on what
you lack, instead try to think of what you can do to get
you out of the situation you're in. Make losing money
into a learning experience and your world
will open up.

Can you:

- Sell something?

- Find a new job?

- Start a business?

- Sell digital products?

- Find something you love to do that can make
  you money?

Unfortunately, I had no idea how to shift my mindset away from catastrophising in my early 20s. So, being made redundant felt like the worst thing in the world. Little did I know, things were about to get even tougher.

Clive and I owed nearly two months' rent. I tried to get another job, but I was so depressed that I couldn't keep one down. One day Clive got alcohol poisoning and had to go to hospital. It was literally one of the scariest moments in my life. I thought I was going to lose him. In truth he did almost die. I don't think we were very good for each other, and although we loved each other, I can see now that our relationship was toxic for both of us.

When he was in hospital, his parents came down and they suggested we both move to Runcorn to live with them. The only thing I knew about Runcorn was it was where they filmed the sitcom **Two Pints of Lager and a Packet of Crisps**. How bad could it be?

💎 Gems of Wisdom

- Don't stick your head in the sand when it comes to money issues. You can't effectively deal with a problem if you don't know what the real problem is, so you need to find the courage to face up to your debt.

- Focus on one positive thing every day, no matter how difficult life feels.

- Whenever you feel like you've failed or something bad happens, remind yourself of the challenges you've already overcome in your life.

- Ask yourself what can you learn from any situation, good or bad? What have you already learned that might help you deal with a problem you're facing now?

Chapter 7

Move Along

> **Move Along *by The All-American Rejects – from their self-titled album***
>
> This song reminded me I was strong, that I'd been through tough times before and that I could move along.

We ran away. We left in the middle of the night, taking only our things, and we didn't give a forwarding address. I owed so much money to the landlady; I didn't know what else to do. I knew it was wrong, but desperate people do desperate things.

I knew I would miss Leicester, but I wouldn't miss checking over my shoulder all the time, for debts and people I really didn't want to see. I felt like I was giving up on my life though.

There was an odd mix of emotions as we stole away in the dead of night. On the one hand, I felt like I was losing my support network by leaving all my friends behind, but on the other, it felt like a chance to put my difficulties behind me; to accept I wasn't a student and to own more of my responsibilities as an adult.

I told myself that a fresh start would be good and that it would be good for Clive to be with his parents. His parents were nice, but I really felt uncomfortable living with them. His brother and sister-in-law were moving out of their flat for a bit and offered to sub let it to us. We jumped at the chance to have our own space.

I went for a job interview for a call centre. They asked me to sell them a pen. I never thought my job at WHSmith would have stood me in good stead for anything, but it turns out not everyone can sell pens! I smashed the interview, and they offered me the job on the spot.

It wasn't the most glamorous of jobs; I was selling gas and electric combined services for British Gas. It was on a dialler, so you had to wait for calls to be put through to you. I spent the time between calls chatting to other people in my team and doodling on a piece of paper.

I loved doodling, it quieted my mind. I'd sketch hearts, stars and trees, sometimes zoning out in a *doodlefart*. Realising how happy it made me, I started selling small doodles for desks, earning a little cash and discovering I was great at sales.

The thrill of a 'yes' was addictive. I built relationships instead of pushing sales, always honest about whether a deal was worth it. My approach worked, I topped the leaderboard, impressed my managers and got promoted to train others. For the first time since being student union president, I felt real purpose, and I was making money!

Clive never got a job. I was supporting him financially, and his drinking was getting worse. I was enjoying making money, and I was finally starting to find my feet. I felt resentment that he was sitting at home all day, often drinking. I knew he was depressed, but I was struggling to be around him. One day I told him that I didn't want to be with him anymore. I went to bed and told him to sleep on the sofa. I knew I needed a better living situation. I told Clive I was moving out.

I packed my bag and went to my friend Mark's house. Mark was a total legend. We started working at the call centre at the same time and he was on my level. He was so kind to let me stay for a few months, sleeping on a mattress on his living room floor.

I couldn't afford to get my own place yet, but at least I didn't have debt collector letters following me around anymore. After a few months, I had finally saved enough money to get a flat. It was grubby and small, but it felt like the first place I could call home.

I needed a new distraction. That was when Bernard (lol) started working in the call centre. We had nothing in common – he was a raving football fan (Everton supporter), and music-wise he liked the pretentious indie stuff I really hated. But he was beautiful. He had floppy brown indie hair and was funny, and I fell for him big time. He was my next hyperfocus.

I spent most of my evenings and weekends with Bernard and I stopped shopping again for a while. When I had a boyfriend, I would get my dopamine from them, as sex was a good replacement for spending. I started working in a pub almost directly over the road from my house, alongside the job at the call centre. I worked hard and played hard. I had some good friends, and I started to enjoy my life again.

Then one day, it started. The letters from debt collectors caught up with me. I thought because I hadn't
heard anything for a year that they didn't know where I
was. But I now had a permanent address, and I didn't
think about the fact that my phone bill was registered to
my flat, so it didn't take long for them to find me. I was
also registered to vote on the electoral roll. How could
I have been so naive as to think they wouldn't find me?

The debt collector's letters came in thick and fast, like
they did before I left uni, but this time there were more
of them. Every day there would be something new.
I felt sick to my stomach. I really didn't know what to
do. I started to trip over my doormat again. The bills
piled up, but I ignored them and filed them in the 'fuck-
it bucket'*. It wasn't that I didn't care, I just didn't know
what to do. I didn't earn enough to pay them and live
the party lifestyle. So, I ignored my debt and prioritised
dopamine and the things that made me happy.

I wasn't an adult yet! I was living a life I enjoyed with a
boyfriend who was FITT! And everyone seemed to like
me here. I was popular. Finally, I had found a place
where I was accepted. Bernard was my world, and I felt
so happy I had someone who I really had fun with.
I didn't realise that I was smothering him.

I made him my world. Because he made me so happy,
I wanted to spend all my time with him. I can see how
wanting to be with him 24/7 would have been a lot for
him to deal with. The thing is, back then I didn't know
how to make myself happy, so I relied on other
people – like Bernard – to make me happy.

If Your Partner Is Neurotypical, Show Them This...

- People like us with ADHD can be a lot, but it's not our fault. We do go all in, and sometimes that can be overwhelming.

- We forget dates, birthdays and planned events. We don't mean to, but we struggle with executive function.

- Ask your ADHD partner how they deal with certain things. There are many amazing ADHD creators out there who talk about ADHD and relationships.

- Don't judge your partner for being messy or disorganised, instead ask how you can help them more.

- People with ADHD aren't lazy. If we don't do what we say we will, please don't punish us.

- Men and women present ADHD in different ways. Remember we are all different and have different struggles. The best questions you can ask are: 'How can I support you?' and 'What do you need?'

One day Bernard told me he needed some space. He had just passed his driving test, and I think as he didn't need me to drive him to work anymore, he felt more able to ask me for space. He had practically moved into my house as it was closer for him to get to work, but once he had his own car, he started coming over less and less. One day he came over and said he was leaving the call centre to get a job closer to home. We stayed together for a few weeks but then he dumped me. The pain was unreal. Rejected, I felt like my life was over...again.

Tips for Healthier ADHD Relationships

- Be mindful of the other person's boundaries. Have an open conversation where you ask them how much they want to see you, and how much is too much when it comes to communicating via text or phone.

- Ask yourself if you're allowing the other person to spend time with their friends and on their own hobbies without you around.

- Reflect on what is making you feel the need to be with them all the time.

- Focus on self-improvement. Find your own hobbies.

- Strengthen your support system. Spend time with your family and friends when your partner isn't around.

- Build confidence and trust in the relationship. When you know your relationship doesn't need constant attention, it's easier to prevent your urge to smother.

- Get therapy or seek counselling if this is something you struggle with.

ADVICE FOR HANDLING RELATIONSHIP BREAKUPS

When you have ADHD and a relationship breaks up, you can feel it more acutely than others because of the rejection sensitivity dysphoria (RSD) you experience, as we've already discussed. I reached out to Claire Standen, a transformational coach (`http://www.clairestanden.com/`) for some advice that might help if you're in a similar situation.

- **Acknowledge your emotions:** Understand that breakups trigger neurological responses of abandonment. There will be a natural grieving process, so give yourself a chance to heal from past or imagined futures.

- **Empower yourself:** Remind yourself that you can provide for your needs. A partner enhances your life but isn't essential for your safety. Focus on your own strengths and independence.

- **Reframe your ADHD as a strength:** Recognise that ADHD brings clarity. If the relationship felt wrong, your ADHD might have helped you see it sooner. Embrace this insight.

- **Redefine success:** Challenge societal expectations about relationships. Measure success by what you've learned about yourself, not by the duration of the relationship. Value your growth and self-discovery.

- **Embrace singledom:** Use single periods to focus on personal goals and dreams. This time is valuable for self-improvement and clarity about future partners.

Managing RSD When It Hits

I find it helpful to 'take the thought to court', which can bring me back into a more rational view of what's happening when RSD strikes. Looking at the facts can help take the sting out of the rejection or criticism.

Take the time to work out how you feel about the situation and to see it from someone else's point of view. Analyse your feelings and perhaps run your thoughts past someone you trust to help you work out whether this is something you should be triggered by, or something that is triggering because of how it's made you feel.

Either way, RSD feels awful in the moment, but always remember this will pass. You've been through this before and survived. You will survive this too.

SLIPPING BACK INTO OLD HABITS...

I was living on my own, I had no boyfriend and my debts were closing in on me. I made myself so sick from crying that I gave myself an ear infection. I called my friend Ian, and he drove me to hospital in the middle of the night. This was when it dawned on me. I was in a strange town, with no family, and my friends all had their own lives. I was heartbroken. And guess what? The spending started again.

I also couldn't understand why another one of my relationships had broken up. It felt like everything in my life had been disrupted, and at this point, I couldn't see that my ADHD was causing my behaviour to be overwhelming – after all, I hadn't been diagnosed.

I didn't have the self-awareness to recognise how my behaviour was impacting others. I also didn't have the self-awareness to see how it was affecting my own life in terms of my finances and health.

Without that awareness, it was all too easy for me to slip back into my old habits of hunting dopamine by spending money on everything from clothes to booze.

 Gems of Wisdom

- Try to find a job that gives you a purpose and that you enjoy, because it will make it much easier to motivate yourself.

- Don't bury your head in the sand when it comes to money worries and debt. No matter how far you run, these things always catch up to you.

- Take some time to reflect on how you show up in your relationships. How can you communicate more clearly and have discussions with your partner to set boundaries you're both happy with?

Chapter 8

Swing Life Away

> **Swing Life Away** *by Rise Against – from their*
> *album* **Siren Song of the Counter Culture**
>
> This is one of my favourite-ever songs. The lyrics
> talk about getting by just fine on minimum
> wage, which feels as though it encapsulates my
> journey at this point where I was just starting to
> get to grips with money and acknowledge that I
> had a problem.

Along with the overspending, the drinking soon
followed. Booze was my crutch. When I was drinking,
nothing else really seemed to matter. It somehow
turned off the constant noise in my head. The voices
telling me I wasn't good enough, that I was lazy and

useless and that no one wanted me here, got drowned out when I had a drink in my hand.

Of course, the more I drank, the more I needed to spend. I spent money to make myself happy, but it wasn't working. I even sought medical help because I knew it wasn't 'normal' to feel this low. The doctors put me on amitriptyline, because of my anxiety and depression.

I'd fallen back into my old pattern of spending, which gave me a high the moment I made a purchase, only to turn to guilt afterwards. I had made some good friends, but this didn't help with my drinking.

On the rebound from Bernard, I was looking for any-thing to make myself feel better. I was spending money, eating unhealthily, drinking and sleeping with people because all these things gave me a little dose of happiness. Temporarily.

I was stuck in a dark hole and the walls felt too steep for me to climb out. I couldn't motivate myself to cook or clean, so I was spending about £60 a week on take-aways. I would go to the supermarket to buy food, but then I wouldn't cook it. I couldn't understand why I wasn't able to 'adult'.

Everyone else I knew seemed to be able to cope with looking after themselves, while I struggled to even do simple tasks. My to-do list seemed endless. The more stuff piled up, the more I felt like a failure. My inner voice kept saying, 'No wonder Bernard didn't want to be with me'. I was lazy and penniless. My brain felt like it was all tangled up, I couldn't think straight, and I had no idea what I was going to do.

Designed by G Sabini-Roberts

By this stage, I was nearly in £40,000 of debt, but I had no available credit, so I was spending my wages and ignoring my bills yet again. I was out of control. Somewhere in my mind I knew I shouldn't be behaving like this, but that voice still wasn't shouting loudly enough to be heard.

My house was full to the brim of crap that I bought when I was hungover. I was also terrible at cleaning, so my house resembled some sort of squat. There were pizza boxes everywhere, unwashed dishes, laundry still in the washing machine (possibly harbouring mould or at the very least damp) and clothes everywhere.

I was still pretending that my debts didn't exist. Until one morning when there was a knock at the door. I was hungover, which was standard for me during this period. I resembled what can only be likened to

Jessica Rabbit on her deathbed – I was covered in glitter, wearing last night's makeup and still had rainbow leggings on, as well as bunny ears.

I didn't want to answer the door. I knew it would be Mel from upstairs, coming to have a cuppa or a natter about something. I felt like I was going to vomit on their shoes – whoever it was. So, I ignored the knocking.

It got louder. It sounded like someone was trying to bash the door down. 'Hang on!' I shouted.

I dragged myself out of bed, put the chain across and opened the door. 'What!!' I answered, a bit aggressively. I was not expecting what happened next.

'Miss Comrie? I'm a certified enforcement officer. I have come to take possessions in place of monies owed'.

The bailiff put his foot in the door so I couldn't close it. Panic ensued and I was sweating alcohol; I could feel it dripping down my forehead. My stomach hit the floor. I definitely felt like I was going to be sick.

I didn't budge, and judging by the state of me he decided not to push it.

'I will be back tomorrow and I'm taking your car', he said, before removing his foot from the doorway and walking away.

What to Do If a Bailiff Shows Up

- Try to stay calm and don't panic. Easier said than done, I know!

- A bailiff can't force their way in, they are only allowed in if you let them. You can say no, especially on their first visit.

- Ask them for ID and ask who the creditor is. Then ask them to have some time to contact the creditor directly.

- If you do let a bailiff in, they are only allowed to take luxury items. They can't take things you need to do your job or to live.

- See if you can get legal advice. This is often offered through your bank or home insurance, so check your policy.

- Don't lie or try to hide things. Also, don't run away. That might seem like a good idea, but they will always catch up to you down the line.

What the fresh merry hell* was I going to do? He couldn't take my car, could he? I could feel the panic rising in me. I called my mum in floods of tears. I blurted out what I had been holding in for five years.

'I'm in trouble mum, I'm in debt, lots of debt'.

I could tell from her tone that my mum was quite relieved. She knew I had been keeping a secret from her, but she thought I was a drug addict, so this was marginally better in her eyes.

'Why don't you come home? We can help you sort this all out', she said.

HOW TO TELL YOUR PARENTS YOU'RE IN DEBT

- **Be honest:** share the full picture, including how much you owe and your repayment plan.

- **Take responsibility:** set a budget or seek advice. Don't expect a bailout – it won't teach you anything.

- **Ask for advice:** involving them shows you're open to support, even if they react poorly at first.

- **Reassure them:** let them know you're committed to paying it off and share your financial goals.

- **Be mindful of money beliefs:** their views may differ, so consider a third-party perspective.

- **Set boundaries:** if asking for help, ensure it won't strain their finances. You created the debt, so own the solution.

ACCEPTING HELP

I wasn't happy where I was. I had no boyfriend. My job wasn't the best. Even though I was good at it, I knew it didn't hold any long-term prospects for me. I accepted that home was probably the best place for me, but I felt so ashamed.

I was scared. I had no idea what was going to happen, but I really didn't want my car to be taken away.

I packed up all my belongings, which took a while. I had more clothes than wardrobe and more shoes than shoe rack. The CDs were all pushed into a big wallet to save space, and I had to rehome my cats.

Rehoming my cats was tough. I loved them, they had seen me through the breakup with Bernard, but I couldn't take them with me. I crammed everything into my car and said a very teary goodbye to all my work friends. I don't think I would have made it without them.

Then I made the six-hour drive to Southampton and cried the whole way. I had left my job, my cats and a boy who I loved but who didn't love me back. I knew my mum was waiting for me at the end of that drive. Although I had told her what happened, I also knew there would be a lot more questions and I wasn't that excited about answering them.

HOW TO SUPPORT YOUR CHILD WHEN THEY'RE IN DEBT

Lesley Thomas, CEO of The Money Confidence Academy – www.themoneyconfidenceacademy.com – has some great advice to parents who find themselves in a similar position to my mum.

- **Listen without judgement:** creating a safe space makes it easier for them to open up.
- **Educate together:** offer budgeting tips or learn about finance as a team.

- **Encourage responsibility:** help them create a realistic repayment plan and an emergency fund.

- **Offer guidance, not money:** help them find financial resources and explore debt repayment methods.

- **Set financial goals:** short- and long-term targets keep them motivated.

- **Avoid bailouts:** paying their debt for them won't teach problem-solving; support them in finding their own solutions.

 Gems of Wisdom

- You can't outrun your financial problems. They will always find you. When they do, be calm and rational. There will be a solution that doesn't involve a bailiff taking your possessions.

- Ask for support from your family. While they shouldn't pay off your debt for you, they can be a valuable emotional support in a difficult period.

- Be honest about your situation. Hiding your money problems from those closest to you only leads to bigger problems later on. I know it's hard, but honesty is the best policy.

Chapter 9

Spiralling

> **Spiralling *by Keane – from their album Perfect Symmetry***
>
> Everything in my life at this point was all-consuming. I had a new job. I had a huge amount of debt to pay off, and I finally realised that I had spiralled out of control. This was when I recognised that I had a problem, and I started to fix it.

As I drove south, I couldn't stop the feeling of dread. I played out the conversation I was about to have with my mum in every way possible, which was something I did in any situation. I always thought that was anxiety but turns out it was autism. I wasn't sure what my plan was. I feared the conversation I knew I was going to have with my mum, but I wasn't sure why because she was always the voice of reason.

I felt like I was the worst daughter and that I had let her down. So rather than going straight to her house, I drove to my dad's. It was my sister Bex's (Rebecca, my sister) birthday, which was timely as I hadn't seen her in a long time. I knew she would help me to de-stress a bit before the horrid stuff I had to talk about with mum the next day.

I couldn't hide from it anymore; it was time for me to grow up. But first, I was going to hang out with my sister. Bex answered the door and handed me a mas-sive glass of vodka and Coke, which was more vodka than Cola.

We had a few drinks at home; then we got the bus into town, where we met up with Bex's friend Sara. I had known Sara since she was 15, and I used to buy her booze at the gig bar when we were younger. She later ended up being one of my bestest friends.

We headed straight for a new club that I had never been to. I remember it being totally Baltic* weather – rainy and windy, standard for January. By the time we got to the club, it was about 11.30 pm. We walked into them playing one of my favourite songs – 'Diamonds and Guns' by Transplants – so I went straight to the dance floor.

In the back of my mind, I knew that I had to go and see my mum in the morning, so I told myself I wouldn't get too drunk. But the large vodka had started me off on a spiral. I was in a place I didn't know, surrounded by music I loved. I started to drink and drink. Although I was with my sister and Sara, I was nervous about being in a new place. I needed to relax, and the shots were 50p each.

I'm not sure how we got home, or even what time. Luckily, my dad was away, because he wouldn't have been happy with what happened next. I woke up to lights being shone in my eyes.

'Maddy! Maddy!' I could hear Bex shouting.

I thought, what in the world of wizardry is going on*? Why am I in an ambulance?

'Has she taken drugs?' I could hear people talking now, but I still had no idea what was going on.

Ouch!!! Someone pricked my finger with something sharp.

'No, she hasn't taken any drugs, she's just really drunk', Bex was saying.

I sat bolt upright. I had no idea what was going on. It turned out my sister had called an ambulance when I started 'acting suspiciously'.

What did I do? I can tell you are dying to know! I had been sleepwalking, something I do when I am really stressed. I had gone into Bex's room, thinking it was the toilet, and done a massive wee in the middle of her carpet! She had caught me pulling my pants down and asked me what I was doing. She had apparently been shouting at me, 'Maddy, stop!!!'

But I was asleep, so I didn't hear her. If I think back to it, I know I was dreaming I was in my old flat. In my brain, the location of her room was where my old toilet was, so it made perfect sense. Bex was not impressed with me!

In the morning, with a very sore head, she made me tell my mum what I had done. In one way, it was a good ice breaker. It gave me something humorous to share to lighten the mood of our very serious conversation. My mum found it hilarious, but it did add to her thinking that I may have had an alcohol problem. She probably wasn't too wrong there.

After we'd all laughed about my drunken antics, my mum sat me down in the living room and I poured out years of stuff I had never told her before. I told her about my spending, about how I never felt like I fitted in anywhere. I said that I was still grieving for her and my dad breaking up and that I was still grieving for the boyfriends I had lost. I told her how I drank to get rid of my problems. I shared how I felt driven by a motor all the time and that I felt like I was addicted to shopping and spending money.

She was cross, of course. I had lied to her for years, or at least been a little loose with the real truth. I think somewhere in my mind I had always known that if I told her, then I would have to stop or change my behaviour. But it was now time for me to face up to the fact that I had a problem with money, although I still didn't admit to myself that I had a problem with alcohol.

During the conversation with my mum, there was a lot of shouting and crying. I tried to defend myself. I didn't even know why I was being defensive – all I knew was I felt like crap. I wasn't trying to make excuses. I didn't know why I had done it. I knew everything I had done with the credit cards, moving and lying was all wrong, but I couldn't help trying to justify myself.

Once we had both calmed down, she told me she loved me, whatever happened. The relief was huge. Then she did the best thing any parent can do in the situation. She said she would help me, but she wasn't going to bail me out.

For starters, she didn't have a spare £40,000 lying around, and she also wanted to help me to learn about budgeting. She recognised that the only way I could learn was by standing on my own two feet.

I am so glad she did. At the time I wasn't happy about it because I just wanted someone to make my problems go away. But I was in £40,000 of debt and no parent should have to pay that. She said I needed to go to the Citizens Advice Bureau and speak to them. So, I booked an appointment.

I wasn't sure what to expect. I was nervous telling a complete stranger about my debts, and I broke down in tears. The situation was very different to the last time I'd sought support from a stranger while I was at university. Looking back, I think the main difference was that at university, I couldn't see a way out, whereas when I moved back to Southampton, I had a job lined up and I knew there would be a way for me to repay my debts.

What I needed to do was reframe my situation, and the person that I spoke to at the Citizens Advice Bureau gave me hope whilst letting me down gently. They said I had two options:

1. Learn how to budget and pay it off.

2. Go bankrupt.

BANKRUPT!! Not a word I wanted to hear. I left feeling as though I only had two options, and both of them were massive. In the years since, I've also learned that I would also have been eligible for an individual voluntary arrangement (IVA), but that wasn't mentioned to me at the time.

What Are the Options for Paying Off Debt?

There are many options for repaying and clearing debt that I wasn't aware of. There are debt management plans, repayment schedules, IVAs and, of course, bankruptcy.

(continued)

A word of warning though: there are many companies that will advertise such solutions online and offer to help you through it. However, what they do is buy the debt from your creditors and then make money from you repaying it to them.

If you are considering an option like bankruptcy, or any other solution that doesn't involve paying your debts back to your original creditors, I recommend you seek advice from the UK debt advice charity Step Change: https://www.stepchange.org/

I didn't want to admit defeat. For one thing I felt ashamed because of the stigma around declaring bankruptcy, and I also felt that it would be much more character building if I paid off my debts rather than writing them off.

I needed to beat the system and do it my own way. Citizens Advice told me about the 50/30/20 rule of budgeting. This is where you spend 50% of your wages on your rent and essential bills, 30% on wants like clothes and going out, and use 20% to pay off your debts every month. I worked out that if I repaid my debt this way, it would take me over 16 years to clear my debts.

I needed a different plan. I am stubborn as a mule on caffeine*, and once I put my mind to something, I do it. I thought to myself: if I do this in under six years, I have beaten the bankruptcy system!

I've since learned that what I'd always considered stubbornness is actually pathological demand avoidance (PDA), which is associated with autism.

Understanding PDA

PDA is characterised by extreme avoidance of everyday demands and expectations due to high anxiety. What this meant for me was that whenever someone told me to do something, it induced so much anxiety that I would avoid it and insist on doing things my own way.

This is different to procrastinating, where you don't want to do something, so you avoid even starting. PDA means you outright refuse to do what you've been told, and you want to do the opposite.

I adapted the 50/30/20 system to be 50/10/40. That meant I spent 50% on my essential living costs like rent and bills, 10% on everyday expenses and food, and 40% of my earnings on paying off my debt to allow me to clear it more quickly.

Give every penny you earn a place. I allocate all my money to different funds. I have a shopping fund, a clothing fund and even a fun fund.

Spend and save intentionally. As long as you plan to spend money on something, it's not an impulse purchase.

I only had my mobile phone and car on finance, and I knew if I went bankrupt, it would leave me without a car. I also knew I wanted to buy a house at some point in the future and knew bankruptcy might affect my ability to do that, so I worked out the least amount of money I could live off to help me repay my debt quicker.

When I was in Warrington, I didn't have a pot to piss in. I was earning money from the pub job to eat, which was about £15 a week. So, I thought if I could live on £15 a week for food and going out, then I could pay these debts back in about five years. Bring it on!

I love a challenge, and somehow I realised that if I gamified the process and challenged myself, I would do it. I considered going bankrupt, but there was so much stigma around it and I felt it would bring shame on my family. What I didn't realise was that no one really had to know. It wasn't as though I would have been walking around with a big tattoo on my forehead saying I was a failure.

It's also important to remember that I was in this situation close to 20 years ago, when the shame around bankruptcy was massive. These days it is fairly well accepted and although it is not a decision you should take lightly, there is a lot less stigma attached to having gone bankrupt.

Is Bankruptcy Right for You?

In some circumstances, bankruptcy might be your best option, but you need to go into it with your eyes wide open to the consequences. Bankruptcy stays on your credit history for six years. But that said, county court judgements and defaults will stay on your history for the same amount of time, so if you already have those, then it may not make so much difference.

If you plan to buy a home with a mortgage in the future, it also might not be the best option for you.

Seek independent advice specific to your circumstances before you make this decision.

In many ways, it would have been a hell of a lot easier to go bankrupt, not that I'm saying bankruptcy is an easy option, but the next part of my life was bloody hard. Although if I had gone bankrupt, I wouldn't be doing what I am now, so no regrets!

> Write down all of your debts, and order them from the smallest to the largest. Make a note of the interest rate you pay on each too. This will help you decide what order to clear them in.

I called all the people I owed money to in one morning, which was really hard, but I knew stringing it out would be worse.

I found the most frustrating part of the process was the waiting – sitting in queues and listening to hold music is the worst, especially when you have ADHD. I think being told you're '17th in the queue…' often puts people off of calling to talk about their debts.

As I write this, companies in the UK – and the people you speak to when you're behind on payments – are a lot more understanding about you needing some time and breathing space now than they ever have been. There are laws in place to protect people struggling with their mental health, money and debts.

Most companies will be happy if you're paying them even just £5 a month and communicating with them about your circumstances. Ask to freeze the interest on the debt and talk to them about payment breaks if you need them.

Communicate with the people you owe money to, because then they won't put pressure on you. It's when you stop communicating that they are likely to call in debt collectors and bailiffs.

I started to hear hold music when I fell asleep. Some of my creditors were really understanding, and others were really unpleasant with me because I had ignored them for so long. I arranged payment plans, some as low as £1 a month.

If picking up the phone is really hard for you, find someone you trust who will sit with you while you make those calls. You can often assign someone to speak on your behalf too, so if you really can't face those conversations, find a family member or close friend who could do that for you.

Often, you'll just need to answer a few security questions, and then you can name the person who can speak for you.

Avalanche vs Snowball Methods of Debt Repayment

I mentioned the avalanche and snowball methods of debt repayment at the end of Chapter 8. Both are equally valid ways of approaching repaying your debts, but I've always found the snowball method works best for me as someone with ADHD, because this gave me dopamine on my journey to becoming debt free. Each time I cleared a debt, it was an achievement and that motivated me to continue.

- **Avalanche:** You pay off the highest-interest debt first, saving you the most money in interest over time. However, this often means you start by paying off your largest debts, which also take the longest to clear.

- **Snowball:** You pay off your smallest debt first, while making the minimum repayment you can on the others. Each time you clear a debt, move the money you were paying towards that one to the next smallest debt and so on.

Give yourself rewards and make paying off your debts into a game. How can you reduce your spend to give you a bit more money to put towards debt repayment? Can you find discounts for your essential purchases?

Tell other people when you clear a debt. This is really powerful and will make you feel even more motivated to clear another debt.

My mum was really patient and helped me to make a budget. Of course, when I left her house, I adapted it so I could still buy things I liked. At the time I had a 20-a-day smoking habit, and I didn't want to stop the boozing. So, I switched from smoking Marlboro Lights to smoking prison rollies, which meant I went from spending about £6 a day on cigarettes to spending £8 a week on a pouch of tobacco.

On the one hand, I wanted to quit, but I also really enjoyed smoking. It gave me a little rush, and I also liked the fact you could take breaks from your desk at work. I needed those breaks because I couldn't just sit and stare at a screen all day, I needed to move about.

STARTING OVER

I had found a job working as a recruitment consultant, and a flat in the middle of nowhere. It was just outside of Southampton in Sholing. I didn't really know Southampton at all, so I didn't realise how much of a pain in the bum it was going to be to get to work every day, especially over a toll bridge.

It wasn't long before I started to get lifts to work with the deputy manager. He didn't like me much. I had to wait for him on the corner of a road nearby, and I was late pretty much every day. My concept of time is really warped. No matter how long I gave myself to get ready in the mornings, I seemed to always be late. A couple of times he left without me, and I was late to work. I don't blame him really; I'm sure it was frustrating.

💡 Tips for Handling Time Blindness

I've gone from always being late to always being early. There doesn't seem to be any happy medium, and I know it's the same for many ADHD ers. Here are a few things I do to make sure that I'm not late and don't forget anything important (like picking up the kids from school!)

- **Set alarms:** I have alarms to remind me of every-thing I need to do throughout the day, so that if I'm focusing on something, I don't lose track of time.

- **Block time or tasks:** Its up to you, I find blocking in tasks helps me to tick them off my list.

- **Use the Pomodoro technique:** This is where you do short bursts of work, followed by short breaks.

- **Stick to a routine:** This can be tricky if, like me, you have ADHD and autism, because my ADHD makes me want to be spontaneous, whereas my autism craves routine. But when you struggle with time blindness, routine is your friend.

The office was small, there were about 10 people who worked there – mostly a bunch of egotistical pricks, but there were a couple of lovely people, including my old boss. When he left the bullying began. I was good at the job and luckily this really helped me to rapidly pay off a lot of my debt.

I managed to get a car through work by choosing a car allowance. This meant I paid a bit more tax than if I'd had a company car, but the car was mine. I bought the most beautiful metallic pink Fiesta.

I earned commission every time I placed someone in a job, and I quickly became the top selling temp consultant on the south coast. Until Alice came along! She was younger and prettier than me and she quickly took the top spot on the leaderboard. I really didn't like her, and I was jealous.

What I've now learned is that ADHD amplifies feelings of comparison jealousy. This means you hyperfocus on someone else's successes, compare yourself to them and then tell yourself you're not as good as they are. My self-esteem took a dip, and I had to work hard to reframe the situation so that I didn't feel so bad about Alice.

For one thing, the area she covered was Bristol, where there are lots of high-volume recruiters. Southampton was a much tougher market. Over time, I was able to bring the focus back to myself. I celebrated my wins, instead of being jealous of hers, and her success inspired me to become better at my job. This was a huge lesson that served me well in the future.

That's not to say it was easy. It felt like the universe had sent her to personally make me feel bad. Of course, Alice had no idea I felt this way. It took me a while to accept that Alice being good at her job was nothing to do with me but was about her own drive to succeed. I also had no support in the office and dreaded going to work every day, which isn't a recipe for doing your best work.

> ### Flip the Script
>
> If you have feelings of comparisonitis, flip the script* rather than being jealous of that person think about how you can be more like them.

UPS AND DOWNS

Recruitment was tough, with many highs but also some deep lows. When a candidate didn't turn up for an interview or they quit soon after starting, I blamed myself, and I started to think I wasn't very good. Alice being better than me didn't help.

I was still getting drunk a lot. I had my five-pint limit on a school night, which would kill me now! I over-shared all the time and would tell tales of my drunken nights out. I thought it would impress people at work, but looking back no one was impressed, they just thought I was annoying.

Still, I was making some nice commissions and every time I got a bonus I would pay a chunk off my debts.

Gems of Wisdom

- Be honest with the people you care about, and who care about you, when you are facing significant debt. Those conversations feel scary, but the relief of sharing the problem is huge.

- Get independent advice to find the best way to deal with your debt based on your circumstances. There are many options besides bankruptcy, so do your research and get support to help you find the right one for you.

- Create a budget and stick to it. Allocate as much money as you can to paying off your debt every month.

- Work out the best way for you to repay debt – the snowball and avalanche methods both work, but one will likely appeal to you more than the other. Choose whichever feels like it will be easiest for you to maintain.

Chapter 10

I Want You

I Want You *by Savage Garden – from their self-titled album*

This song resonated with me as I struggled with wanting to buy everything but needing to be strict with my spending. The lyrics that hit home: 'Oooh I want you, I don't know if I need you, but I would die to find out'.

I moved to Bedford Place, which was where my office was, and I spent my whole life living in a triangle. Work, pub, home, work, pub, home. Nothing was more than 100 m away from anything else. Through Facebook, I discovered that Rach, my best friend from school, lived just up the road.

We had drifted apart during our time at university, but when she posted to say she had broken up with her boyfriend of five years, I messaged her to say if she ever wanted a chat or a drink, I was only down the road. She messaged back straight away and said, 'I'm free tonight'.

It was like we had never been apart. We went on a bar crawl, and then we were inseparable. I spent most weekends hanging out with her. We faced our own challenges but always supported each other. I can't put into words how much I appreciate her friendship. She is always striving to better herself, and I have always admired that.

Having a close friend made all the difference. Rach moved into the flat above mine, and I felt less alone. She is still one of my best friends to this day.

I started working for the bar below my office passing out flyers for them on Tuesdays and Thursdays for a bit of extra cash. Mainly this job involved going round all the pubs and talking to people. It was cash in hand, which meant I didn't get taxed. So, I used the cash to pay for food, and I had more money to focus on paying off my debts.

I was still binge drinking a lot and my whole social life centred around the various bars and pubs Rach and I would frequent. It's not uncommon for those of us with ADHD to focus on substances like alcohol, drugs and even caffeine to give us a dopamine hit, help quiet our minds and make us feel 'normal'.

Personally, alcohol gave me false confidence and helped me feel like I fitted in socially at this point in my life. I'm not sure who was the bad influence here, me or Rach! But we had a lot of fun.

My Southampton life consisted of going to work, then going to the pub then going home, I was focusing on repaying my debts, I knew the thing I had to change was my shopping habits. I still needed to shop – I needed that dopamine hit. By this point, I had realised I had a problem, but I didn't know how to tackle my spending, so I just bought cheaper items.

Your Food Budget

- Search for discounts: you'll find discount vouchers on *Mad About Wellbeing* hub.

- Switch to non-branded food.

- Look high and low in supermarkets for cheaper items and avoid the ends of aisles that are designed to make you spend more money.

- Use ChatGPT to help you work out what you can make with discounted items.

- Keep an eye out for the yellow sticker sections in supermarkets.

- Freeze stuff: Kate Hall's book **The Full Freezer** is a great resource.

- Set a realistic food budget; to do this, you need to work out your entire budget.

I went to the supermarket seven days a week and yellow stickers became my new addiction. I used to stalk the guy who marked up the reduced items as he moved around the store to see what he was scanning.

We became quite friendly, and he used to scan the stuff I wanted to reduce it for me! I also found a love for charity shops. I got my dopamine fix finding designer clothes and selling them. Or I kept and upcycled them with my sewing machine.

Cutting Back Sustainably

Sell things you no longer need, especially things that don't give you joy. Check out the charity shops and car boot sales, and Facebook Marketplace when you want new clothes.

I loved being thrifty and my debts started to go down quickly as a result. I sold stuff online, so I had a bit more money to live on and any time I got more money I paid off more of my debts. I hyper focused and I had to learn to say no, which was hard.

I also found budgeting boring, so I allowed myself a spending pot to still enjoy life. What really helped me stay on track was seeing budgeting like a game – it's one I was good at. I mainly focused on scrimping on food and clothes.

Have 'No Spend' Days

I have at least one day a week where I am not allowed to spend any money. This can help you become more mindful about money.

I still bought CDs, but I learned more about downloading music, and that helped me save money too. I had cut my debt by half – huge progress – and I felt great! The debt collectors' letters had stopped, and I was on top of things.

Every time I received a big bonus, which was often, I would pay off another chunk of my debts. It was hard living on £15 a week for food, even 15 years ago when things were very different.

Sometimes I would go days without eating – not that I'd advise that. Despite my erratic eating habits, I was still pretty big as my body seemed to cling onto fat for dear life.

When I was eating, my food choices weren't great, and I was piling on the weight. The gin-and-pizza diet is not one I would recommend.

I was the heaviest I had ever been. I felt rubbish about myself, I didn't feel attractive. I felt like my weight directly reflected how I felt about myself. When I feel overweight, I feel stuck, which demotivates me and prevents me from working towards my goals.

Nowadays, I am probably the largest I have been, but body positive and not nearly as obsessed with how my weight is.

I opened up to one of my friends about how unhappy I was with my weight, and she suggested I join one of those slimming clubs. You know the ones I mean, they're like a cult that preys on people who are trying to better themselves. I found a lot of the rules around what I could and couldn't eat were a saucepan of poopoo*. I mean you can eat as many bananas as you like but if you mash them the world catches fire! I did find the accountability was helpful and I started to slowly lose weight.

Accountability is really important when you have ADHD because it gives you a sense of validation that you're not the only person going through a challenge. We need cheerleaders who praise us to keep us motivated. This praise is also another way we can get a dopamine hit.

Free Ways to Get a Dopamine Hit

- Receiving praise or love.

- Hugs (if you want them).

- Cheerleading others and giving compliments.

- Exercise, like going for a run or a walk.

- Reading a book.

- Watching Netflix.

- Hanging out with friends

One of the best ways of introducing more accountability into your life is to find your people. That might be a Facebook group, a local community group or your friends and family. The key is to own who you are and to find other people who have things in common with you or who are facing similar challenges. Like my membership programme **Invisible to Influential**, where I hang out every day.

Get Accountable

Talk to the people around you. Tell them you are trying to reduce your spending, and it will help you to stay on track.

At this point in my journey, I felt like I was finding my feet. I was earning good money in a job that I quite enjoyed. I had a couple of really good friends. I had found ways to make saving money and budgeting more fun. And I was making great progress in paying off my debts. For the first time in a long while, life felt a bit more stable. I would never have foreseen the earthquake that was coming.

Gems of Wisdom

- Create a budget and stick to it. If you still find you're overspending, track your expenses for at least two weeks by writing down everything you spend money on. This will help you work out where you are overspending. I find adding what you are feeling when you spend money helpful too, like happy or sad or bored so you can track patterns.

- Avoid unplanned purchases as they make it harder to save.

- See if you can find other ways of making money around your main job to give you some extra cash.

- Build up a support network who can help you stay accountable for your goals.

Chapter 11

End Transmission

> **End Transmission** *by AFI – from their album*
> **Crash Love**
>
> This song is all about being free and starting out
> on the right path. It symbolises my shift in
> mindset around my money.

Our team at work had performed really well for the
quarter, so our boss bought us all a picnic in the
office. There were sandwiches, cake and plenty of
other bad foods that I was trying to avoid. I said thank
you, but that 'I didn't want anything as I was
on a diet'.

A short while later, I went out for a cigarette and my
boss stepped into the lift with me. As we went back

upstairs, he told me he thought it was silly that I wouldn't eat any of the picnic. So I told him I was trying to lose weight and that I'd already lost over a stone.

I got back to my computer and started working, not thinking much about it. Suddenly, my boss barged me away from my computer. He was tapping away on my keyboard furiously – as though he was trying to diffuse a bomb. I couldn't understand his behaviour as he'd never acted like this before.

As though reading my mind, he turned to me and said, 'I sent you an email accidentally'.

The rest of the office was snickering, and when I returned to my computer, there was nothing in my inbox. What was so important he had to barge me out of the way to delete it? Surely, he could have just told me what he'd sent? Something fishy was going on, and I needed to uncover it.

I waited for him to go out to get our afternoon coffees, then put my detective hat on. I called the IT department and got them to retrieve the email. I wish I hadn't because it turned into a catastrophuk*.

It was an email my boss had sent to my team, including the person I was managing. It read, 'Maddy just told me she has lost two stone...' and a picture of a blimp.

Canva

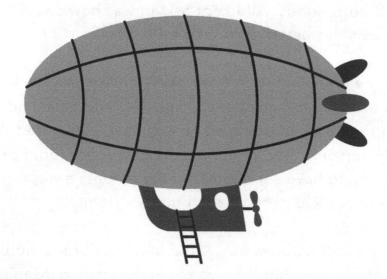

He called me fat to my whole team. I have never been
so hurt or embarrassed. I had always known that
I wasn't the most popular person in the office, but
I didn't realise I was the butt of everyone's jokes.
I couldn't understand why people were so mean.

My boss knew I had retrieved the email, and he asked
me for a chat. He was shaking and white as a sheet,
likely because he knew he could have easily lost his
job. I was still in shock and didn't know what to say. He
told me to take some time off and decide what I
wanted to do. I walked out crying.

I went home, got under my duvet and did nothing but
think about it for two weeks. I loved that job. Even
though most of the people were horrible, it was helping me to make massive debt repayments. I had a
company car, and I had respect from the senior managers. But how the hell could I carry on working there

after that?! My boss was essentially pushing me out. I felt horrendous. All I kept asking was how could someone I trusted do this to me?

I'd been humiliated in front of my colleagues, including the people I managed. I knew I could have had him fired and, in doing so, would have eliminated the only person ahead of me for the manager's job. I probably could have sued him. But my parents always taught me two wrongs don't make a right.

After a couple of weeks, I told him to stick his job up his arse, asked him to give me my month's gardening leave, and walked out. I was totally bricking it* mind you. Although I never felt like I fitted in with that job, I hated change.

I was still in £20,000 of debt, and I knew I didn't have long to find something else. Maybe leaving my job was an overreaction, but I couldn't work with people who were spilling tea that's all about me*
behind my back.

Dealing with Change

When you understand that you don't like change, and that something changing will throw you off, it can help you to manage your emotions
around change.

With change comes grief and loss, so it is important to reflect on how change impacts you and how

(continued)

it makes you feel. Even when a change is good, it can still make you feel uncomfortable. Knowing that you'll feel uncomfortable before it happens can help you process your feelings.

Looking back, it was a huge betrayal of trust and the final nail in the coffin in an environment where I already felt as though people were talking about me behind my back. It massively knocked my self-esteem and made my rejection sensitivity dysphoria (RSD) really flare up too. It only got worse when none of them turned up for the leaving drinks I organised.

Put Together an RSD 'Go Bag'

Can you create a list of things which help you feel better and give you dopamine/distract you? Or create a sentence for yourself such as: 'When I recognise I'm experiencing RSD, I will … to help myself feel…'

Your go bag might contain a book you love, a song that makes you happy, a healthy snack or even someone you trust on speed dial. This doesn't have to be a physical bag, it can be a mental 'bag' too.

ADHD Coach Charlotte Dover, of `https://charlotedover.com`, also shared this helpful advice for when you experience RSD:

- RSD is NORMAL in ADHD.

- Sharing how it feels with friends can help them understand.

- It will pass.

- Name it to tame it.

- Treat yourself with compassion through an attack.

- Remember you're loved.

- RSD lies; it's based on interpretation not fact.

 Gems of Wisdom

- Unexpected events will happen in life that might feel like they can throw you off track. If this happens, don't beat yourself up. You will find a way through the challenge you're facing.

- Dealing with change can be difficult, so give yourself time and space to process what's happening and to grieve for what you've lost.

- RSD can flare up for many reasons and it's a normal part of having ADHD. Find your own ways to cope with it so that you can put things in perspective and prevent it from derailing you.

Chapter 12

What It Is to Burn

> **What It Is to Burn** *by Finch – from their album*
> **What It Is to Burn**
>
> Once you've read this chapter, you'll understand
> the full significance of this song. But I also
> chose it because it is in the intro of my
> favourite-ever programme, One Tree Hill.

I struggled to find another job. Nothing seemed right.
Every day I was going on recruitment websites and
hunting. I couldn't sign on because I couldn't bring
myself to do it, mainly due to the number of forms and
paperwork. I was always so bad at forms and anything
admin based.

Offload Your Admin...

I'm being serious. If you really hate admin to the point that you don't do it, outsource as much of it as you can. I talk about this all the time on my *TikTok* channel. Find someone on Fiverr or Upwork who is organised and pay them to do it for you. This doesn't have to cost a lot. There are cheap ways to take these things off your plate.

I searched for about six weeks. I had no prospects. I felt so worthless. How could I have been so good at the last job, and now no one wanted me? I felt paranoid. I began to think I was not as good as I thought. My good old rejection sensitivity dysphoria (RSD) kicking in again!

Flip the Script on RSD

Remember that RSD and feeling rejected usually comes from the meaning we assign to something which has happened, which isn't always the truth of the situation. We are often our own harshest critics, which can mean that we experience RSD from our own thoughts about who we are and what we are (not) capable of. This is often not the truth! Try to find facts/proof of situations where the opposite/positive has been true about yourself.

I've found that it's helpful to journal about opposites/positives, so that when my RSD flares up, I can look back at

(continued)

what has helped me in the past. These can be positive words or thoughts. Always ask yourself, how can I flip the script?

I finally got an interview with a company that sounded amazing. They offered me a £35,000 basic salary, which was a £5,000 increase from what I had made before. Jackpot! They had been our biggest competitor, and as soon as they found out I was available, they offered me a job.

But here's the catch. They wanted me to bring all my clients over – it's recruitment, so it's cut-throat. I managed to bring in some, but I started to get legal threats for breaking restricted covenants, which was scary. My new employer told me that I had to carry on anyway. It was uncomfortable, but I continued to push.

This affected my mental health. My social life had dropped off after I left my job mainly because I wasn't working a stones throw away from my local pub anymore. I felt like I had lost a group of friends, and I was still focusing on budgeting. I was spending more time at home and focusing on my new boyfriend, Edgar (hehe). He was funny, kind and got on with my friends. And as it turned out, he literally saved my life. It all started with an accident...

I hadn't been in the new job long when Edgar had a serious accident, which put a huge strain on our relationship. To celebrate his recovery, we went out with friends and got really drunk.

At 3.30 am, Edgar woke me up. 'We have to get out! The flat's on fire!!!' I looked out of the window, and I could see flames. I could smell smoke too, I was terrified. We ran out and bumped into Helen, who lived next door. Then we searched around for other people we knew from the block.

My friend Dave who lived upstairs had been out with us, but he was nowhere to be seen. I panicked. He hadn't heard the alarm! It was so loud now that I was up, but I hadn't heard it either – it was such a good job Edgar was there!

We told the firemen about Dave. They were pounding on his door, but no luck. We stood outside watching as the whole roof of the flats just went up. It was so scary.

All of a sudden, I realised I had left my phone inside. I hadn't had time to pick anything up. But that was the least of my worries. We still hadn't seen Dave.

The firemen finally got Dave out by squirting him through his window with water, which woke him with a shock. We all cheered as he came out, but we were all in shock. We waited outside in the cold until 5 am when a local pub opened their doors, so we had somewhere to wait indoors.

LOSS AND SOUL SEARCHING

I was wearing a long t-shirt and a dressing gown, and as I sat down, it suddenly dawned on me that I wasn't wearing any pants – genuinely the first time I was panty-less in a pub! I didn't have my wallet or any money on me. Luckily, the owners of the pub were kind and gave us hot drinks and bacon sandwiches. It was a long day. We were finally told that we couldn't re-enter the flats, because it was too dangerous, so we had to find alternative places to stay.

I thought I could stay with Edgar, it would just be for a few days, right?! How wrong was I! When we went back the next day to see the state of play, I was told that my flat was one of the worst affected. The flat that was on fire was directly above mine so everything I owned was ruined by smoke and water damage. We still weren't allowed in, so I didn't know how bad it was.

It took four long days before they secured the flats enough for us to be let in. One of the guys working on the building told us we'd need wellies. 'Wtaf? Wellies?! Why?!' I asked. Luckily Edgar had the same sized feet as me, which said a lot!

'You will see when you get in', he replied. We walked up the stairs to my second floor flat. The floor was squelchy, and we were ankle deep in water. When we opened my door, the smell was horrific.

I could see my phone on the side. I took it. It wouldn't turn on, but I knew I could fix it if I bagged it with some rice. Now I knew what the worker had meant. My bed had a lake in the middle of it. I genuinely thought I would see frogs jumping up and down on it and the smell made me think wildlife had inhabited the place. My sofa had already started to get mouldy.

None of my electronics worked. All of my personal things from old diaries, gig tickets and photos from university, to posters and letters I had kept from school, had turned to mush. I was devastated. My memories were gone. I'm incredibly sentimental, so to see the things I had been collecting for years ruined beyond repair was the worst part of it for me.

Weirdly though, this also showed me how unmaterialistic I am. I didn't care about my shoes, bags, clothes or most of the things I had spent so much money – and accrued so much debt – on buying. I did a lot of soul searching.

I had experienced a massive loss, and I grieved for my stuff, but what I realised was that none of the 'stuff' really mattered. I'd spent most of my life buying stuff for the dopamine hit, but the items themselves weren't important. What was important was that we were all ok. I was safe, my friend Helen was safe, Dave was safe. We all got out alive, and no one was hurt.

I was so lucky to be alive, but I didn't feel very lucky. I kept wondering why I was such a chaos conductor*? I felt like I was cursed. But the fact is, this was

just life. BUT ADHD life and I was still bliss-
fully unaware.

The cause of the fire turned out to be a BBQ that the
students who lived in the top floor flat had left running on the roof. Drunken Morons!

THE VALUE OF PROTECTION

Now is the point when I talk to you about protection.
No, not that kind! Get your minds out of the gutter! I
mean insurance. Having contents insurance is probably the one thing I did right in my adult life. Without
it, I would have been beyond screwed.

I'm not exaggerating when I say that having
contents insurance saved my life after the fire. I managed to claim £15,000 back for all of my stuff – I still
thank my lucky stars I was insured. In fact, having
so many designer clothes from my days at university
and my charity shopping came in handy
with my claim.

I had to make a list of everything I had lost. That list
contained items from some expensive brands and by
some miracle, the value of my claim added up to
£15,000. This was almost exactly what I had left
of my debts.

I was grateful to be alive. Even though I'd lost some
really important stuff, I had realised that a lot of my
possessions weren't that important to me after all.

So, with most of the insurance payout, I paid off my last £14,000 of debt.

It felt absolutely amazing. It simultaneously felt like the biggest achievement of my life, while leaving me without a purpose. I had spent so long hyperfocusing on paying off my debt that it felt weird when it had gone.

There was a weird dopamine lull in my life after achieving something so significant. I started drinking more because my purpose had suddenly vanished. I didn't know where to put my money. It took me a little while to figure out what to do next, but eventually I shifted my focus from paying off debt to saving.

REBUILDING MY LIFE

I used the £1,000 left from my insurance money to rebuild my life, although it turns out that £1,000 doesn't go all that far. I was free! But I was also depressed. Not only had the fire made me homeless, it also made me jobless.

I had taken a fair amount of time off work due to the fire and Edgar's accident, and the company said I wasn't a team player. It was their loss, but it didn't feel like that at the time.

They didn't even pay me the £4,000 commission I was owed. I was also still living at Edgar's, and I knew I needed to act fast. I headed to Rightmove and started searching. All of a sudden, there it was, just what I needed – the flat I had shared with my friend Tim a few years earlier.

It felt like it was meant to be. I loved that flat – although it was more like a house with two up two down. It was over a shop, which was pretty handy for hangover food and milk. And it was also a really good flat for parties, especially in the summer.

I didn't hesitate. I called the landlady, whose number I still had from when I lived there before, who was more than happy to rent it to me directly. Less than a week later I moved in. It was needed as life with Edgar was getting intense. We were certainly not ready to live together, and I needed my own space.

One problem solved – I wasn't homeless anymore. But I knew I couldn't last without a job for long.

It was time to throw myself back into job hunting, but nothing felt right. I interviewed for a few things, and I even considered going back to the recruitment job I'd chosen to leave after the email incident. But then I'd remember how hurt I felt after no one showed up to my leaving drinks and I'd keep searching.

Not long after I moved into my new flat, Edgar dumped me. Looking back, I think he was waiting until I was back on my feet – at least he didn't make me homeless. He said he didn't want to get married and didn't want any kids, but he knew I did, and said it wasn't fair on me. Even though I knew on some level we weren't that compatible, it still hurt, a lot.

I wasn't out of the woods with grief and pain just yet, it seemed!

REBUILDING YOUR CREDIT RATING

I also knew I needed to do some work to rebuild my credit rating after paying off the debt. It's a long process as your credit rating takes a battering when you miss payments. If you receive a county court judgement or debt relief order, it'll take you longer to improve your credit score because those things can stay on your record for up to six years.

One of the best ways to start rebuilding your credit score is to take out something on credit that you know you will always pay on time. I'm talking about broadband or a mobile phone, nothing excessive.

Keep your utilised credit low too, so if your credit card has a £1,000 limit, keep your borrowing to £500 or less. I also recommend checking your credit report regularly as this will give you tips on how to improve your score.

- **Boost Your Credit Score**

- **Totallymoney.com:** free credit score tips.

- **Join a credit union:** access small, affordable loans to rebuild credit.

- **Try Loqbox:** a reverse loan that boosts your score while helping you save.

Rebuilding your credit score can be a bit of a minefield. It's also worth remembering that hard credit searches will impact your credit score, so if you're looking for something like insurance that will require a credit check, make sure it's a soft search.

 Gems of Wisdom

- Take out contents insurance for your possessions. It was a life saver for me.
- When you finish paying off your debt, look for ways you can rebuild your credit score.
- Find a purpose for your money once you pay off all of your debt. Could you switch to saving at least some of the money you were using to pay off debt and build up a buffer?

Chapter 13

The Middle

> **The Middle** *by Jimmy Eat World – from their album* **Bleed American**
>
> This has been one of my favourite songs since I was about 17 years old. The lyrics 'Don't write yourself off yet, it's only in your head you feel left out or looked down on. Just try your best, try everything you can...' really spoke to me at this point in my life.

To deal with the pain of my latest break up, I reverted to behaviour that I knew. The next few weeks were spent drinking way too much rose wine, smoking way too many cigarettes and only leaving the house to go to work or the pub. I had formed a rather neat little triangle between my new job, the pub and my house again. My new job was working at another recruitment agency.

I knew this wasn't my forever job, and I told myself 'beggars can't be choosers'. I didn't enjoy the job itself, but I did make a friend there, Karla, who I'm still friends with to this day. She made the days at work bearable with our banter. Everything seemed to be going OK...

ANOTHER SETBACK

I'd had my smear test around the time I started in my new job, and a few weeks later, I received a letter telling me they had detected pre-cancerous cells. This wasn't actually the first time this had happened to me – I'd had this twice before and needed two rounds of laser surgery when I was 19 and 25 years old.

But this time it was more severe than the last, and I was told I needed to have some of my cervix cut out.

A Friendly Reminder

For all the cervix owners out there, this is your friendly reminder to have a regular smear test. Is it unpleasant and at times painful? Yes. But trust me when I say it's worth it to save you future issues – take it from someone who's had several issues with their inner secret garden!

(continued)

When you have a neurodivergent condition, the pain of these kinds of procedures can feel worse because we tend to focus on it more than neuro-typical people do, but that's not an excuse to avoid the appointment!

What a bastard!

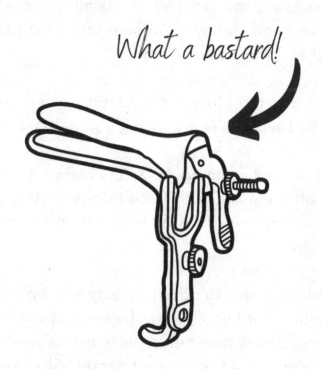

Barely two months into my new job, I had to tell them I needed an operation. It was early days, but I was doing ok at the work and had placed a couple of people. I didn't foresee taking time off for a medical procedure being an issue.

After the operation, I had to take a few days off to recover, and I went to my mum's so someone could look after me. It was a long few days. The doctor told me that it would be very unlikely I would be able to have children, and if I did get pregnant, it was very unlikely that my cervix would let me carry a baby to term. I was heartbroken.

All I had ever wanted was to have kids. I was super maternal and learning I would be unlikely to have one of my own made me very sad. It was a lot to deal with and so I was completely unprepared for what happened when I went back to work.

I was called to the office for a meeting, where they opened by saying: 'We are giving you a disciplinary'.

My mind started spinning. WTAF!? I knew I had been a bit slow off the mark, but I hadn't done anything wrong. I was confused. As if I wasn't going through enough already!

They told me it was to do with a lady who I placed in a job claiming that I had lied to the company about her. Total farce. I think they heard the word 'cancer' and thought 'nope, not playing that game!* She's going to be off sick too much . . .' so they found a way to get me out.

Once again, I found myself jobless. My critical inner monologue started up again. Why did all this stuff always happen to me? I was definitely stuck in victim mode, I felt like yet again my world had come crashing down. I seemed to be a professional misstepper* everything I touched. I was struggling with life so much, and I still had no idea why.

ADHD AND THE STRUGGLES WITH EXECUTIVE FUNCTIONS

People who have ADHD struggle with executive functions, which are controlled by an area of the brain called the *prefrontal cortex*. This part of the brain integrates the inputs from several brain regions and allows us to pay attention to what is most important at a given time, as well as to carry out various other executive functions.[1]

These executive functions are what we need to be able to function like a neurotypical adult. The problem is, it affects basically everything. These are just some of the most prominent examples:

Working memory: I can't remember what I had for breakfast today, let alone something someone asked me to do last week. I can't remember people's names, which I always find the most embarrassing. I forget my friends' birthdays, even if they are written in my diary.

Inhibitory control: I can't control my impulses. If I think I have to do something, I just do it without thinking of the consequences – you may have noticed examples of this in the stories I've shared so far. I have foot-in-mouth disease – although I can also blame autism for that. I say it like I see it. My knack

---

[1] Wilcox, K., PhD (2024) 'Understanding the neurobiology behind ADHD behaviors', **Psychology Today**, 17 September. https://www.psychologytoday.com/us/blog/mythbusting-adhd/202409/unlocking-the-adhd-brain

for overspending and distractibility could also be included under this inhibitory control umbrella.

Cognitive flexibility: This involves the ability to switch between tasks effortlessly. I find changing from one thing to another really hard. Even a simple action, like getting out of the car when I get home, can take me ages. I often sit for 5–20 minutes psyching myself up to go inside. A tip for this is put the hot blowers on, then you will get so dysregulated you have to go indoors!

Going to bed is also challenging. I literally need my husband to body-double me going to bed and to eat food. When he isn't here, it's more challenging to look after myself and I often forget to eat, stay up late and spend hours scrolling on *TikTok*. I haven't mastered this yet, so if you've got any advice for how to improve this aspect of your life when you have ADHD, I'd love to hear it.

Planning and organisation: I feel like the least organised person on the planet. I forget times, dates and I double-book myself all the time. Luckily, my clients often do as well, and they have a sense of humour about it.

The Menu System for Organisation

I've come up with a way of managing my time and ensuring I complete important tasks. I call it the menu system. It's very simple.

At the start of each day, I write five different tasks on five different Post-it notes and stick them to the

(continued)

wall. Those are my tasks for the day, but I don't beat myself up if they don't get done and I can carry them forward if I need to. This really helps me to remember to do those mundane, everyday tasks (like invoicing) that I would otherwise easily forget.

Time management: I'm either five minutes late for everything or half an hour early. Being on time is not something that exists in my world. Check out the tips in Chapter 9 if this is something you also struggle with.

Emotional regulation: 'She's so emotional'. 'Cry-baby'. 'Oh, temper, temper'. 'Stop overreacting'. 'Drama queen'. All of these were phrases said to me as a kid. I struggled to control my emotions, I still do. When I was a child, it was a daily struggle, and I had no clue why.

Charlotte Sharp, MBACP/DIP Accredited Counsellor (www.charlottesharpcounselling.co.uk) shared some great tips for emotional regulation when you have ADHD:

By Charlotte Sharp, MBACP/DIP (charlottesharp-counselling.co.uk)

- **Move daily:** exercise boosts dopamine and helps regulate emotions.

- **Be mindful:** walk, listen to music, or observe your surroundings to stay present.

- **Know yourself:** tune into your feelings and self-soothe when needed.

- **Brain dump:** journaling clears mental clutter, no perfection needed.

- **Reflect weekly:** rate your stress (1–10) and spot burnout signs.

- **Try water therapy:** cold showers can reset your nervous system.

- **Take your time:** allow extra processing time for emails and decisions.

- **Watch your sugar intake:** dopamine spikes lead to crashes and dysregulation.

All of these factors made my life really difficult, and the hardest part was not understanding why I couldn't just 'be like everybody else'. When I was younger, I didn't know ADHD existed in women, let alone that I had it. I know that's a common issue for many women and it's one of the many reasons I've written this book. If I've helped you make sense of your life, then I've done my job.

Maybe I've helped you self-diagnose, or maybe I've just shown you that you aren't alone if you find any of what I've talked about challenging too. Whether you have an ADHD diagnosis already, think you might have ADHD or are just curious, all I'd advise is to focus on your own journey. Give yourself the space to understand and learn about your own brain and how it works.

When I lost my job at the recruitment agency, my journey of self-discovery took another turn.

Gems of Wisdom

- Don't avoid appointments like smear tests, they can literally save your life. It can be easy to forget to book them in, but make it one of your daily priorities when you get the letter.

- Take some time to think about what you struggle with in life. If what I've said so far in this book is resonating with you, it might be an idea to get your own ADHD assessment.

Chapter 14

Weightless

> **Weightless *by All Time Low – from their album*
> Nothing Personal**
>
> All Time Low are my favourite band. 'Maybe it's
> not my weekend, but it's going to be my year'.
> That line has got me through so many dark
> times and reminds me that when I feel like I'm
> not on the right path, success is just around
> the corner.

I knew I was brilliant at recruitment, but I didn't want
to work for someone else again. I was done with feeling unvalued and unwanted. So, I decided to strike
out on my own and start a recruitment agency.

I knew I was meant for something different, but what should I call my new business? Something quirky. Something me! Enter **Purple Cat Recruitment** – a name choice I later massively regretted.

I designed my own logo in Microsoft Paint (yes, you read that correctly – what was I thinking?!), and my friend Dave designed a website for me. How anyone took me seriously I have no idea! I had zero knowledge of marketing, or how to run a business. How hard could it be?

As it turns out, really hard.

Research shows adults with ADHD are six times more likely to be an entrepreneur than those who are neurotypical.[1] This makes perfect sense – we tend to be impulsive. So, I went from thinking 'I'm good at recruitment' to 'I'm going to build a recruitment business' without considering any of the consequences or any of the ins and outs involved in actually running a business. I didn't think about the admin I'd have to do if I was working on my own, the software I'd need to buy, the specific qualifications and insurance I'd need or the fact that big businesses want to work with big recruiters – not one-woman bands. And the truth is that I actually really didn't have enough passion to do recruitment as a business.

---

[1] The Economist (2012) 'In praise of misfits', *The Economist*, 2 June. https://www.economist.com/business/2012/06/02/in-praise-of-misfits

Find Support

If you're planning to set up your own business, get some help to make sure you know what's involved and don't make the same mistakes I did (there were many, as you'll see!). That's why I started my membership community – to help other people with a neurodivergent condition lay the foundations for a successful business.

THE REALITY OF STARTING A BUSINESS

It didn't take long for the hard reality to set in after my initial excitement. The first thing that I struggled with was motivating myself. I had no money and no clients. That meant I had to sit with the Yellow Pages and cold call companies, something that I utterly detested.

Facebook had just started offering 'pages', so I set up a Facebook page with my snazzy (who am I kidding, it was crap) logo.

Shortly after, a tin pot company gave me a job vacancy to fill. I filled it using my Facebook network and the local paper where I chucked in a £30 mini advert. I got paid £700 for filling that job and I thought I had made it!

My initial euphoria soon wore off. With the money I made, I paid for access to Reed so I could search for CVs, and I kept cold calling.

What motivated me to keep going? The fact I had no money to pay my rent or bills certainly helped. I may have been debt free, but I was still hunting down the yellow stickers in the supermarket, and eating concoctions of the weirdest food known to man. I was totally and utterly broke.

The other thing that kept me going in those early days was my grandpa. He was an entrepreneur and someone who I admired greatly. He made his millions in a massive deal for lighting for an international project, and I wanted nothing more than to be like him.

I knew I wasn't going to make my millions working from my bedroom with a half-broken laptop. So, I rented an office that was equidistant from my house and the pub. It was empty, so I had to source furniture. My dad lent me some money, and I went on the search for purple chairs, a purple rug and a desk.

I wanted to look the part when candidates came in to see me, so I also rented a water cooler! When I look back now, of all the pointless junk I could spend money on, that was the worst. Picture the scene: a small, freezing room, with two purple tub chairs, a black and purple rug, a desk and a water cooler. Terrible. I lasted just six months in that office.

Reality began to bite. Clients who I used to work with wouldn't work with me because I was too small and much as they liked me, their procurement teams just wouldn't have it. I was low and struggling. I didn't enjoy going into work, mainly because I hated what I was doing.

💡 Tips When Starting a Business

Plan: A business plan is essential for starting a business. Always remember the quote 'fail to prepare, prepare to fail'. Winging it with a business just doesn't work.

ICO registration: Register for the ICO (Information Commissioner's Office). This is essential if you are processing data of any sort. It will cost you a maximum of £60 a year.

Insurance: Purchase business insurance. It's boring, but necessary.

Be online: If you are thinking about starting a business and you are not happy to show your face on camera, I'm sorry, but it's going to be bloody hard to sell anything.

Data storage: You'll need somewhere to keep your data – a CRM or similar. You might be able to get by with a spreadsheet to start with.

Space: If possible, work from home. Even if you need space for your business, spend your first three months, which is when you create your plan, working from home to save costs.

Website: Opt for a simple website. WordPress or Wix will do, or even Go High Level where you can build multiple websites and landing pages for under £100 a month (at the time of writing).

Explore social media: *TikTok* is great! My advice is to get out there and start growing an audience organically. It's totally doable! (I know a great *TikTok* coach if you want some help – me!).

RISKS AND SELF-EMPLOYMENT

Taking risks is a natural part of life, but it's important to recognise that risk-taking is a part of your journey to working for yourself and to acknowledge that those risks are different to the ones you face if you're employed. The following are a few things to watch out for if you're going down the self-employment route as someone who's neurodivergent, courtesy of Mahmood Reza of I H8 Numbers: `https://www.ihatenumbers.co.uk/`

Be prepared: self-employment is different from a job; plan for challenges.

Set boundaries: your business will impact your personal life.

Know the trade-offs: you get freedom and rewards but take on more risks.

Save for quiet periods: work isn't always steady, so build a financial cushion.

Plan ahead: running a business without a plan is like sailing without a compass.

Get paid on time: set clear payment terms, invoice promptly and chase late payments.

Expect slow growth: it may take two to three years to establish steady income.

Manage cash flow: budget for ongoing costs like subscriptions and insurance.

Price correctly: don't undervalue your work; cover costs and make a profit.

Avoid over reliance: diversify clients to reduce risk.

Track finances: review income, expenses and profitability regularly.

Understanding Financial Terms

Working capital just means the amount of money your business needs to be able to operate on a day-to-day basis.

Cash flow is simply the movement of money in and out of your business.

Beware of Burnout

It's particularly hard to manage these boundaries when you have a neurodivergent condition and love what you're doing. You'll want to work all the time – I know I would work myself into the ground if I didn't have really strict boundaries for myself. I've worked in a perpetual cycle of burnout in the past, and although initially that seems fine, trust me when I say it isn't productive or healthy.

Nobody else is going to run your business for you, so take care of yourself.

It's About Where You Focus, Not How Much You Do

One thing I've learned over the years is that success in business doesn't come down to how much

(continued)

work you do, but to where you focus your efforts. You need to have a solid plan to ensure that you're focusing your energy on the right places. Working with a coach can help ensure you put your focus where it's needed

Productivity doesn't mean doing all of the things, it means doing the right things.

Every Penny Counts – Stay Focused

- When you start your own business it's even more important to keep an eye on your personal finances. Use penny roundups – that just means every time you make a transaction you can round the amount up to the nearest pound and all those pennies go into your savings.

- Name your savings – give your savings pot a name so you know what you're saving for. If you've labelled your savings for a specific purpose, you're less likely to take money out of them for something else.

- Don't feel guilty for spending your savings – if you're using your savings for the purpose for which you saved them, don't feel guilty about that. It's why they're there.

- Don't hoard money – remember money is a flow. Don't hoard it just because you can save, save intentionally and with purpose.

Planning Tips for Those with ADHD

Planning is really hard when you have ADHD, so simplify it. I have created a business plan template for my *Mad About Money* community, which helps you to break bigger tasks down into small steps. Your business plan is like your road map. It needs to answer questions like:

- What's your purpose?

- What are your values?

- What's your mission?

- Where are you going to carry out your business activities?

- What are your strengths, weaknesses and opportunities?

As expected, I was very easily distracted during that time. I would be distracted by sounds, people, smells, pretty much anything – although at the time I didn't realise quite how distracted I really was.

But my biggest distraction was my grandpa getting sick. He had cancer, and while that wasn't what killed him, it helped him on his way. He was the strongest person I knew. He was a giant – 6'7" – and I used to call him the 'BFG'. He used to chase me and my sister around the house pretending to be the Pink Panther. I loved him so much and he was my rock during my parents' divorce. He was always so patient with me.

In August 2012, while I was in the midst of getting my recruitment business off the ground, my grandpa caught pneumonia and passed away. I vividly remember when he died.

I was at Reading Festival – with a backstage pass I'd managed to wangle through my radio connections. The day started amazingly. I met Simon Pegg and Fearne Cotton. I have to be honest, Fearne triggered my RSD for years. She seemed to have the life I wanted. But she was so lovely I instantly felt guilty that I'd been so jealous of her for so long. The highlight of my whole day was meeting Jack and Alex from All Time Low, my favourite-ever band.

Then the energy changed. I was already feeling like something was wrong that day, but then I had an overwhelming sense of impending doom. This, plus free beers for an ADHDer with no off switch, was not a great combination. I decided to drink for England*.

Foo Fighters were headlining, and by the time they took to the stage, I was a mess – a drunken shamble. At some point, I lost my phone, my wallet, my keys and most definitely my dignity. I left the festival in a drunken state, without my friend Dave who I'd gone there with.

Gems of Wisdom

- Be aware of how your neurodivergent conditions will cause you to take risks and think differently about setting up a business. Thinking differently can be a platform for success, as long as you get your foundations in place.

- Understand that you'll likely be distracted, so create a clear plan and get a business coach to ensure you focus on the activities that will move you forward fastest.

- Don't expect the world on a stick. You can become a successful businessperson, but it doesn't happen overnight and you need to put the time and effort in. Steady, sustainable growth is the way to go.

Chapter 15

Patience

> **Patience *by Take That – from their album* Beautiful World**
>
> I'm a massive Take That fan and this song felt like it perfectly summed up what I went through when my grandpa died. It's all about needing time to process things that happen and the importance of giving yourself time and space to grieve.

The morning after Reading Festival I had the worst hangover guilt. I felt awful for leaving Dave behind. I had no phone and no wallet. It was incredibly lucky I had a spare key under my mat; otherwise, I wouldn't have had anywhere to sleep. I woke up feeling terrible; then my house phone started ringing.

It was my mum, 'Grandpa died last night darling', she said. My world came crashing down. My sense of impending doom and the change of energy suddenly made sense. I didn't stop crying for about a week.

My hero, the man who I looked up to the most, had gone. I hadn't really ever had anyone this close to me die before. I was broken.

His funeral was a week later, just after I returned from Bestival with the girls. With grandpa's funeral looming, I had gone on another drinking binge, which was kicked off by a tarot card reading, during which the lady said 'Your grandpa is watching out for you, you will start seeing signs'.

I walked out of the tarot reading, sat down on a hill and started to cry.

Someone dressed as the Pink Panther came and put their hand on my shoulder, 'Everything will be alright, just trust in the process', the Pink Panther said, and then walked away. That gave me an instant terror surge*. It felt like my grandpa was talking to me via someone else.

At this point, I realised I was on my own and had no idea where the girls were, so I started to drink more. I got lost and ended up drinking the night away with someone dressed as Jesus. My friends weren't impressed with me when I turned up at 6 am the following morning.

They forgave me but disappearing like that. Causing them so much worry was one of my biggest mistakes – all due to my inability to stop when it came to booze.

THE HARDEST GOODBYE

Grandpa's funeral was the next day. I was still hungover. I had been drinking pretty solidly for a week. I never saw myself as an alcoholic, but I definitely had issues with drinking. Even though I could go weeks without it, as soon as I had a drop I couldn't stop.

We all went into the church for his burial. I was glad it wasn't a cremation. I hated the idea of him being burned, and I also wanted to know I could walk on him, sit with him and see his grave. Since then, there have been so many times where I have been to talk with him, especially when things haven't been right in my business. He still helps me even now. The ceremony was hard. I struggled to control my emotions. I sobbed and cried more tears than I thought I had in my eyes.

Morning has broken – more like Maddy is broken. It was literally the worst day. They played his favourite song, *Feelin' Groovy* by Simon and Garfunkel. Seeing his coffin getting lowered into the ground, it felt like my heart was getting ripped from my chest.

People threw in roses, his favourite flower. I threw in Liquorice Allsorts. I was worried people would see me as being disrespectful, but I'm glad I did it because it meant something to me and to him – we used to sit and munch on them when my grandma wasn't watching and to this day the little bobble ones give me all of the dopamine.

I got some looks, but we had such a special bond, it was our thing.

I'm crying as I write this. He was such a big part of my life. Things just haven't been the same since he left. But I have always vowed to do things in a way that would make him proud.

If there is an important decision to be made, I always think 'What would grandpa do?'

I know that grandpa would be proud of me and the things I have achieved, and I often think about him. I wish he was around now to see how I have changed my life around.

FINDING YOUR WAY THROUGH GRIEF

Grief comes in many shapes and forms. It's sadness, anger, regret, longing, frustration – there is a whole mix of feelings involved, and those feelings are hard to understand at the best of times when you have a neurodivergent condition. What I've learned from my experiences is that it's important to give yourself time and to understand that you're going to go through almost every emotion possible.

It probably would have helped if I'd talked to a professional at the time, rather than the Pink Panther on a
hill at Bestival. There is a bit more on grief later
in the book.

Gems of Wisdom

- Grief comes in many forms, and it doesn't just
  'go away'. Understand what you're feeling and
  where it comes from and accept it.

- You'll have your own way of finding comfort and
  consolation during this time. Whatever that is –
  whether it's going to church, having tarot read-
  ings or something else – lean into it.

- Daily rituals can really help. Find one that works
  for you and stick to it.

Chapter 16

It Must Be Love

> **It Must Be Love** *by Madness – from their album*
> **Complete Madness**
>
> I was very much starting to love myself. After my
> grandpa died, I really discovered what I already
> knew – that I was different – and embraced that.
> The old saying, 'You won't find anyone to love
> you until you love yourself', is very true.

James (real name this time) had been a friend for a
long time when my grandpa died. Although he eventually became my husband, at this stage, our relationship was purely platonic. I was busy grieving my
grandpa, starting my own business and getting over
the cancer scare. I was overwhelmed. Nothing I did

helped apart from talking to James. He was such a calming influence.

He saw me for who I was, and I felt like I could be honest with him about everything; he never judged me. It was the first time I had ever felt like I really mattered. He was going through some stuff as well, and we just clicked. At the time, I didn't know James was the right person for me. But it turns out that he's the best thing that ever happened to me.

I was honest with him about my money situation from day one, and he told me he saw money as a partnership when you are in a couple. I had never had this before and he made me feel safe. We shared all the same values, and we even spoke about how we would parent together, and how we would split household chores if we moved in together.

He supports me emotionally, especially in the run up to my period I am an unstable basket case! I struggle with PMDD, which is premenstrual dysphoric disorder (more on that later). James is super supportive, and I am very grateful that I've found someone who is there for me in this way.

One of the biggest things James and I had in common was our music taste. His music collection was one to kill for – I only really had two options, kill him for it or marry him – clearly, I chose the latter! We also both share a love for rugby – our first date was to see a rugby match at Twickenham – we both like live music and we really enjoy hanging out together.

I realised I loved him pretty early on. I can't explain it other than that there was just something really different about him. He was kind – the sort of kind where you know someone would walk through fire for you; the sort of kind where I knew he would look after me, not as a carer but on a more supportive level. Although a lot of the time he does end up being my carer! I am not sure I would be a functioning adult without him!

Over the course of six months, we got to know one another better and our feelings for one another evolved. But during this time, I was also focusing on building my business and navigating my way through my grief after losing my grandpa.

BUILDING A NETWORK

I received some inheritance from my grandpa, and I spent some of that money on the office. I also started networking. I joined a networking community, where the networking breakfast cost £15. That seemed so extravagant at the time, given that £15 would usually feed me for a week! Even though getting there was a struggle, I loved networking. You wouldn't know it because of how sociable I am, but I get very nervous in business situations. This is common among those of us with neurodivergent conditions, especially if we have autism.

Once I was into the networking event and chatting to people I felt more at ease, but I would sit outside in the car for about half an hour psyching myself up to go in. This is what's called 'transition paralysis' in the

ADHD community. Essentially, it means that you struggle to shift from one task or environment to another. ADHDers can find transitions mentally exhausting or overwhelming, so we need this time to mentally prepare and decompress. In a weird way, it's a form of self-care, where we're protecting ourselves from an unknown situation.

Everyone in the networking group was supportive, but as a small business owner I never felt like I really belonged. It was very corporate and formal. I didn't feel like I was a proper business owner, I had no idea what I was doing and I certainly had imposter syndrome. That said, this network kept the business afloat for a good six months, although I was still only making minimal money.

I rarely met anyone who could help me to make money. It was only down the line that I realised networking is all about building your network. You don't go into these events to sell your services, you go to these events to make connections, help people and, in return, get help. It's all about support and friendship, so it's only after a long time when you really have nailed your niche that it will start to pay off.

ACCEPTING THE TRUTH

As you have probably gathered, I did everything on a budget in my business, and the sign outside the office was no different. I designed it myself and it had a big purple cat with a curly tail on it, the business name – *Purple Cat Recruitment* – and my mobile number. Every weekend, for months, I would receive five or six calls from people asking how they could get into the brothel, what services I offered and how much I charged.

Yes, that's right, people saw my sign and thought my business was a front for a brothel. The final straw was when my local newspaper ran an article about the recruitment agency that everyone thought was a brothel. It was hilarious, but also incredibly embarrassing. I couldn't carry on.

It was time to face facts. Purple Cat Recruitment was dead. In truth, it was never really alive. Although I was ready to let go of the business in many ways, the thing I struggled most with was that I'd poured money from my grandpa into it. I had tried to put the money he'd left me to good use, and I'd failed spectacularly – although I'm sure he'd have found the reason I closed my business hilarious if he'd still been around to hear the story.

At the time I felt like a failure, and my RSD hit me quite deeply because I felt I hadn't met societal expectations. I hadn't been diagnosed at this stage, but I now know it's important not to blame yourself when things don't work out. When you have ADHD, you have executive dysfunction and challenges with regulating your emotions, so don't be too hard on yourself. And remember everything you do is learning and preparing you for the next step.

Accept Your Brain Is Different

Understand and accept that your brain works differently to neurotypical people's brains. You will feel and process events and emotions differently so show self-compassion. Find a way to flip the script and reframe your negative thoughts.

I always come back to 'Everything happens for a reason'. I know that if something fails, life has a better purpose for me just around the corner.

I find it helps to think of life like a soundtrack. If you were to listen to your past soundtrack, you'd find songs on there that no longer resonate. You might even find that the tape unravels in places and that you need to wind it back in to reset. You can rewind, listen to past tracks and learn from them too. You can press pause and take a break. You can fast-forward old tracks to get back to the latest one.

Think of all of the ups and downs in your life as different tracks on your mixtape. They all mean something different, but that doesn't mean you have to listen to all of them on repeat.

Over the years, I've realised that life is about being a serial blunderer*, fixing it and learning to do better. That's the cycle we all go through. Sometimes we'll screw up in a big way, other times it'll be something smaller.

As I said, I'm a big believer in everything happening for a reason. Purple Cat Recruitment wasn't my dream or my purpose. The problem was, I didn't know what was. I started job hunting again.

Advice to Avoid Wasting an Inheritance

These tips come from Vix Munro, founder of Retire Rich: retirerichwithvix.com.

Pause first: Take time to process emotionally and financially before making decisions.

Make a plan: Align your inheritance with your life and financial goals to avoid impulse spending.

Tackle debt: Prioritise paying off high-interest debt to reduce financial stress.

Invest wisely: Learn the basics of investing to grow your money long-term.

Enjoy some: Set aside a portion for fun – life is for living!

Get support: A financial coach or advisor can help manage a large inheritance.

SEARCHING FOR A PATH

I was hired by a small executive search company to help them to set up a recruitment arm. They had big ambitions, but they wanted someone who was corporate, and I just didn't fit that mould. I tried my best to conform, but I wasn't the right person.

I made money for them, but they refused to accept that to launch a new business, you needed some form of online presence – we didn't have any. I asked for a marketing budget, but they didn't have one. I think they expected me to launch a massive recruitment agency because of my experience with nothing other than my charm. I did ok, but it was too much pressure. I lasted about six months before moving on.

So, the job hunt continued. I found a new agency, which already had two branches and wanted to open a third. They took me on as the manager. No clients, no contacts, no systems. I set up the whole thing.

Then they fired me three months later because the branch wasn't making enough money, and their over-heads were too high. They offered my job to the lady I recruited under me who had only eight months of experience. Unsurprisingly, she didn't do any better.

At this point, I was done with recruitment. But I still hadn't figured out that I was part of the problem – because I hated recruitment, I don't think I was trying my best in any of these jobs. Instead, I told myself, 'Maddy you'd do better if you applied yourself'.
In reality, all I was doing was masking how much this was affecting me because I didn't want to appear as though I had failed again.

I was fooling myself that I was working hard, but I was depressed and struggling to cope with undiagnosed ADHD. Everything was hard. I just didn't know why. After suffering rejection so many times, I started to feel really crappy. All I kept asking myself was: 'Why am I so unemployable?'

I did a series of temporary jobs for a bit, which I really enjoyed. The variety was interesting, and the money wasn't too bad, but just as I started to feel settled something would change, and I didn't like change.

Finally, I got an interview for a different type of recruitment, internal. No more competition, no more fighting over commissions, no more cut-throat.

My interviewer was super successful and terrifying. She was the sort of person I really wanted to be. I think it was one of the hardest interviews I have ever done, and I was shocked when she offered me the job.

I started a week later. On my first day, I met Gary, Dangerous Dave, who was also new, and Ellie. They were all really nice, down-to-earth people, and it helped that they also seemed to be into the same sort of music as me. They felt like my people, and for the first time I was working in an office where I had real friends. The job itself was incredibly boring, but the people made it fun.

The account that was meant to be on was for a big IT systems company, but the contract hadn't started when I joined. So, I ended up recruiting for a delivery company contract for a few months while we waited for that IT account to start.

The stories I could tell you about delivery drivers who temp! It was crazy and it was hard to recruit them. The rates were so low it was almost more favourable to be on benefits, and people didn't want to do the driver jobs. I started just before Christmas, so volume was key.

People would get sacked daily, so the work to find people was erased as they left, as was all the dopamine in my body. It was a very unfulfilling job.

But I had my goal in mind – to work on the new contract when it came in. However, my work on that contract was delayed even further as there was so much admin to do for the setup. Even though I found the delivery contract hard work, I knew I had to stick with it. I needed the money.

Eventually, I got started on the IT systems contract, but little did I know that my life was about to change again, in a very dramatic way.

 Gems of Wisdom

- Talk about your challenges with managing money with your partner. It is always best to be honest about these kinds of issues from the start.

- Networking can be great when you're building a business – but remember that you need to build relationships before you sell anything.

- Everything happens for a reason. We all make mistakes, and we all fail sometimes. The key is to learn from mistakes and focus on the opportunities in the future, rather than fixating on what's happened in the past.

Chapter 17

Feeling a Moment

Feeling a Moment *by Feeder – from their album* Pushing the Senses

This song is all about being grounded, understanding when something in your life is changing and, instead of panicking, sitting with it and taking time to work out how to deal with a completely unexpected situation.

The lead up to Christmas was pretty boozy, and I was going out with my new friends a lot. During this time, I was also in the process of buying a house. A lot was changing in my world – new job, new home, moving in with James, Oh and we also impulsively bought a dog. We named him Dexter, because he seemed to tear everything to shreds if left unsupervised for more than

3 minutes. If dogs can have neurodivergent conditions, he most definitely had all of them. Yes, he is a spaniel.

All of the changes were positive, but they also felt quite stressful. Those of us with ADHD often don't like change, and the stress of change can mean that we lose control of our financial situation.

So, it's important to find ways to help stay on track with your money, even when you're facing a lot of changes in your life. Even though this can also be a challenge for neurotypical people, people with neurodivergent conditions tend to feel overwhelmed by change more frequently in their lives.

When you have ADHD, traits like impulsivity, forgetfulness, difficulty with long-term planning, overspending, not budgeting properly and being disorganised with paying bills can all result in financial instability, so we have to be very mindful when we notice that change – or the prospect of change – is tipping the balance the wrong way. Even positive changes in your life can throw your money out of whack, so it's important to check in regularly.

How to Stay on Track with Your Money Management

- Use financial tools, apps and communities for support (like the *Mad About Money* app, which is available in then app stores).

- Simplify your financial life. Get rid of anything that doesn't matter (go back to your budget and look at your priorities).

- Get into a routine. Choose dates you will remember like the first of the month to pay your bills or have your monthly money date.

- Automate your payments for important bills.

- If you're moving house, the TransferMyBills (`transfermybills.com`) app is great. It changes your name and address over for you, so it's a great way to cut out the kind of admin our brains hate doing.

- Break your money down into categories or pots, so you can see them visually.

- Use visual aids like physical spreadsheets.

- Be accountable by having open conversations with people around you.

- Use a body-double to motivate you to pay your bills. There is an awesome app called *dubbii* created by the lovely Rox and Rich from ADHD Love that can help with this; it also helps you keep up with essential daily tasks like washing and laundry.

- Consider using a money coach.

BUYING A HOME

I had managed to save enough money for a deposit for a house and I had some inheritance money left from my grandpa, but my credit rating was still awful from all the years in debt. That meant getting a mortgage was a tough gig.

I decided to get a shared ownership place because the deposits were lower (5%), although due to my credit rating, I had to give a 12% deposit to get the mortgage over the line. Even then it was touch and go! I remember getting the call to say I had been accepted. It was nothing short of a miracle! I genuinely feel like I manifester it!

Tips for Saving to Buy a House

- Think about your budget and how much you can afford. Without a budget, you won't know what level of mortgage repayments you can afford each month.

- Set goals. Work out how much you need for a deposit and put money aside each month.

- Speak to a mortgage broker early on to find out how much you'll be able to borrow.

- Work out what you can sacrifice to save the money. Bear in mind that underwriters will want to see what you're spending your money on before they give you a mortgage, so expenses like a weekly take-away are some of the first you should cut.

- Shop around for the right deal and check the interest rate. You can find deals for head credit, but you will likely pay a lot more in interest.

- Pay your deposit savings into an account like an ISA that you can't withdraw funds from without a penalty. This helps prevent you from spending your savings on mindless crap.

I bought this house off plot, which basically means it was an apple in the developer's eye and building work hadn't even started, and this was incredibly stressful. I had to wait about seven months after being accepted to move in. By the time moving day rolled around, just before Christmas, I had already decided James was coming with me. Even though it was my house, I knew he was my person.

He accepted me for who I was, he said he had never met anyone like me. He still stands by that now, 13 years down the line – he knows I am proudly different and proudly neurodivergent!

MOVING IN

Finally, we got word that the house was 'ready'. I say ready in inverted commas because it was far from being ready! We basically moved into a building site with a snagging list longer than the Magna Carta. I'm pretty sure some of the stuff that was on there still hasn't been done 10 years later!

We moved in on 17 December. It had been a mission to get everything in before Christmas, and we were far from unpacked. James' mum, Jenny, came to stay with us. She was wonderful, very kind and loving and accepted me into her family. But when she arrived, it was clear she was unimpressed that we hadn't fully unpacked the kitchen. With the house resembling an organised dumping ground, we decided to go out for dinner.

I ordered the seafood pasta, minus the scallops, which was delicious, and we had a lovely evening.

But the next day was vomit central. I couldn't figure it out – the food was great and no one else was ill. Was I allergic to seafood now? I was really poorly, and Christmas became a write off.

By the day before New Year's Eve, Jenny had gone home, and I had started to feel a bit better. James suggested we go to the new Hugh Fearnley-Whittingstall restaurant, River Cottage, in Winchester (which sadly doesn't exist anymore). We had amazing but very rich food, and afterwards, I felt *really* sick.

On the way home, I told James that I thought I was pregnant. I had never felt this sick for so long. We stopped off so I could grab a pregnancy test – being a money saver, I picked the cheapest one on the shelf. Once we were home, I peed on the stick (and my hand), waited the required two minutes, and . . . not pregnant.

Great, I must be dying, I thought.

The next night was New Year's Eve, and we met all of our friends at our favourite pub, The Cricketers. One of my best friends, Helen, had been off the booze for a bit because of a course of antibiotics. When I got to the pub, another of our friends, Stokes, bet me £5 that she wasn't drinking because she was pregnant.

'No way', I told him, 'She would have told me if she was'. We shook on it and then Helen arrived with a massive glass of red wine in hand.

'Ha! I told you!' I turned to Stokes. Helen looked amused as he reached for his wallet. 'What's all this about?' she asked.

'He bet me £5 that you were pregnant', I replied, holding my hand out to Stokes for the cash.

'Well, looks like you owe him a fiver then. This is non-alcoholic!' Helen said with a grin.

It took a minute for the penny to drop. I was so happy for her – one of my best friends, pregnant! But, at the same time, I felt a little sad. After my cancer scare, I knew there was next to no chance that I would ever be sharing that kind of news with my friends.

I excused myself and headed to the toilet, I started crying; then I threw up. The room started spinning and, for the first time ever on New Year's Eve, I was at

home and in bed before Big Ben chimed midnight.
I could hear all the fireworks going off outside, but I
felt so poorly that I couldn't get up to watch.

NEW YEAR, NEW ME, NEW BULLSH*T

I went back to work the next week still feeling rubbish,
but I'd decided to start a health kick. I challenged
myself to drink two litres of water a day – when you have
ADHD remembering to drink water is hard. I stuck to
my two litres a day, but I was peeing every 15 minutes.

My boss even told me off for going to the bathroom
so much. Everything was agitating me that day. I took
myself outside for a cigarette and then walked in
Eastleigh, which we affectionately called 'Beastly'.
The best part about it was all the charity shops.

I had even started to set myself a weekly charity shop
budget. It was my way of staying on top of my spending but still getting the dopamine from the shopping.
I wouldn't always spend my weekly budget – it was
only £5 – but I always rolled it over if I didn't spend it.

Other Tips for Shopping Without Spending (Too Much) Money

Here are some other techniques I use to get a
dopamine hit from shopping without breaking
my budget:

- Try pretend shopping, where you put an item in
  your online basket and then leave it. This takes a

lot of willpower. If you still really want it after a week, set yourself a goal to save the money you need to buy it.

- Go bargain hunting – sites like Vinted are great for finding items at bargain prices. If you've got your eye on an expensive piece of clothing, a handbag or another accessory, see if you can find the same thing cheaper elsewhere. I get a great dopamine rush from bargain hunting!

- Spend consciously. It can be tempting, especially around Black Friday or January sales, to buy things you don't need. Even if you have the money available, if you don't need it, don't buy it.

I bought a couple of books from the charity shop and went back to the office. As soon as I walked in, I nearly vomited on the floor! What was that god awful smell? Someone about four banks of desks away from mine was eating an orange. Then another guy walked out of the kitchen carrying a freshly microwaved fish pie. The combination of the two smells made me want to hurl – but how could I smell that when they were both so far away from me?

That night I got home and decided to take the other pregnancy test that was in the box I'd bought before Christmas.

Negative.

I was feeling miserable and couldn't understand why I felt so sick. The week dragged, but I'd only been in this job for about eight weeks. I was too scared to ask for a day off.

By 7 January, I had been feeling sick for over two weeks. I ran a bath in the hope that it would make me feel better. While I was in the bathtub, I suddenly remembered reading an article about the line on pregnancy tests not always working.

I called out to James and asked him to get the pregnancy test I'd taken a day earlier out of the bin. We both studied it. Was there a line?

THIN BLUE LINE I asked James to go out and buy another test. This time he bought a Clear Blue one – which is probably what I should have bought in the first place. I peed. We waited.

Pregnant. No freaking way*!!!!! I was actually pregnant! I burst into tears!

Then I instantly started panicking about how much booze I had drunk and how many cigarettes I'd smoked over Christmas. I was happy but really confused – I wasn't supposed to have kids. I didn't think I could after my cancer scare. Then my mental monologue started – I'm happy, but I haven't finished living my life yet. I can't even look after myself. Oh my god. I'm going to be the worst mum ever.

When you have ADHD, your brain always goes to the worst possible scenario – we disasterbait*. We catastrophise because of the way our brains process emotions, and this can also lead to emotional dysregulation. All of this becomes a cycle, where we feel so overwhelmed by future problems that we catastrophise further. I looked at James, he was really happy. I think I was still in shock.

Tips for Dealing with Major Life Changes When You Have ADHD

- Be realistic and understand that change takes time to adjust to.

- It's normal to feel anxious about things changing, especially when you have ADHD. I get stressed out about the smallest of things, like changing my route to school or when they change the packaging of my favourite food. What I learned is that having a baby will throw you, but you do find a new groove.

- Look after yourself where you can and be kind. Don't beat yourself up.

- It's normal to feel anxious about a really big change – like having a baby – but you will cope (and you'll be a good parent!).

- Plan as much as you can. This will help take the burden away on the days when you don't feel in control.

Having a baby is a particularly massive change. You go from just being you and your partner to having something screaming and crying around you 24/7. Not that I want to scare you if you haven't had kids yet, but this does create extra stress in a relationship. Make sure you talk about your coping strategies together and how you'll deal with conflict when the baby comes.

At least I finally knew why I had been feeling so terrible. Not that it was much consolation. My morning sickness was horrendous – I felt like I was going to vomit 24/7 for 15 weeks. As I have a phobia of sick, I was constantly on edge. It was stressful, and I felt like I wasn't in full control.

My next thoughts were about work – I'd finally found a place where I enjoyed working, even if the job was boring. I had friends there, and we had a laugh. What was I going to tell them?

 Gems of Wisdom

- Managing change when you have ADHD is hard, and it can throw you off in such a way that good habits you've developed go out of the window. Be kind to yourself, but also be aware that change might make you more forgetful than usual. Do what you can to stay on track.

- Recognise that some chaos fuels productivity and use your periods of hyperfocus to your advantage.

- Get into good financial habits and stick to them, no matter what. Use some of the tools I've shared throughout this book to help keep you on track.
- If you're saving for something big, like a house deposit, set yourself goals. Do some research to work out how much you'll need to save and use that to motivate you to put money away regularly.

Chapter 18

Learn to Fly

> **Learn to Fly *by Foo Fighters – from their album* There Is Nothing Left to Lose**
>
> This is mine and James' song. But boy did it feel like I had to learn to fly all over again when I was pregnant.

Initially, I wasn't sure if I should tell my new employers about the pregnancy. I had told Laura, my work bestie, and she knew how terrible I was feeling. In the end, I told my boss at about 12 weeks – in fact, I didn't have much choice. I vomited all over myself and my desk, which was super embarrassing. It felt good to get it off my chest though as I'd felt like I was harbouring a massive secret.

As it turned out morning sickness was the least of my worries. At 14 weeks, I was tested for gestational diabetes – basically diabetes that lasts while you're pregnant – and, of course, I had it. I had to do a finger prick test every day and later in my pregnancy I had cravings for sweet things that I wasn't allowed to eat – I have the worst sweet tooth and hate needles. Typical.

Not only was I terrified of being a mum and didn't feel ready to give up my party lifestyle, I was now getting zero dopamine because I couldn't have my sweet treats.

I had to be super careful what I ate. I was grumpy and I felt awful for my whole pregnancy. But gestational diabetes wasn't even the worst of it. I'm hyper mobile, which is fairly common for those with ADHD, and while I was pregnant, one of my ribs just casually decided to pop out! Agony! But worst of all, I started to itch.

I felt like I had thousands of tiny insects crawling all over me, especially at night. It was unbearable, especially when accompanied by dagger crotch (which basically feels like someone is literally stabbing you in the foof with a dagger), restless leg syndrome and pelvic girdle pain. It's safe to say I wasn't getting much sleep.

The itching got so bad that I went to my doctors and was diagnosed with obstetric cholestasis, yet another piece of fruit to put in the bowl*! This time one where your liver struggles to transport bile acids. It's vile.

THE REALITY OF PRENATAL DEPRESSION

Given all of this, it's little wonder I felt depressed. People talk about postpartum depression a lot, but prenatal depression is barely mentioned. I hadn't even had my baby yet, and I was about as depressed as they come. I thought I was going to be a terrible mum, and it felt like I wasn't coping. Hormones were raging through my body faster than an F1 racing car.

Interestingly, prenatal depression has been identified as a risk factor for your child developing ADHD. One study found that women who experienced prenatal depression were three times more likely to have a child who was diagnosed with ADHD than those who didn't experience depression during their pregnancy.[1]

ADHD affects our emotional regulation, sensory processing and attention focus, which is also why ADHDers like me become so consumed with things like morning sickness. We hyperfocus on discomfort, and when that's combined with heightened sensory sensitivity, it makes what we're experiencing feel overwhelming and all-consuming.

We also have difficulty regulating our emotions, so we struggle to manage the feelings of frustration, stress and sadness that go alongside feeling sick. And we

---

[1] Nidey, N.L. *et al.* (2021) 'Association between perinatal depression and risk of attention deficit hyperactivity disorder among children: a retrospective cohort study', *Annals of Epidemiology*, 63, pp. 1–6. https://doi.org/10.1016/j.annepidem.2021.06.005

have a low tolerance for having our routines disrupted, so when we're ill and can't do what we normally would, we'll find it disproportionately frustrating.

I was showing up to work groggy and feeling like crap every single day. The job was hard as there was a lot to learn for the new account. I felt like I had cotton wool between my ears. I was so tired that there were times when I fell asleep at my desk.

I struggled with the half-hour drive to work every day, and I was working until 9 pm most nights. There was a lot of organisation and attention to detail within my role, and there was way more admin than I'd antici-pated. I found it really hard going and didn't under-stand why I struggled so much with tasks everyone else found simple.

But I had to stick it out and work there through my pregnancy to get maternity pay. I was lucky that I'd been there just over 12 weeks when I realised I was pregnant, as that meant that at least I qualified for maternity pay. Seven months went by.

My pregnancy was horrid. My life was ruled by injec-tions and finger pricking. I was so low.

I felt sick; I couldn't eat what I wanted. I wasn't even looking forward to the baby coming. The pregnancy was stealing my joy. I couldn't tell anyone how I was feeling. I felt so ungrateful, especially when so many people want babies and can't have them. I knew I was lucky, but I didn't feel it.

I had a sense of constant guilt, which wasn't helped by the fact that society tells you to be happy when you're pregnant. I worried that I wouldn't be able to take care of my child properly – I just kept thinking that I could barely look after myself so how would I look after a child? My future felt very uncertain, and that only exacerbated the lack of control I was feeling.

If you're in a similar position, all I can advise you to do is focus on your own well-being. It's paramount. Relax and minimise stress as much as you possibly can. Have baths, do exercise and try to eat healthily – I want to be very clear; I didn't do any of this. Instead, I ate what my brain wanted to eat – strawberry laces were one of my biggest cravings until the gestational diabetes diagnosis meant I wasn't allowed them anymore.

But I think when you're in this kind of situation, you have to give yourself permission to do both. Find whatever helps you through.

PREPARING FOR THE BABY ARRIVING

As soon as I found out I was pregnant, I started to put money away for when the baby arrived – just £20 a week into my savings. That wasn't enough. I really didn't anticipate how expensive having a baby would be.

How Much to Save for a Baby?

- Aim for **3–6 months' living expenses** to ease the impact of low maternity pay.

- Calculate the gap between your maternity pay and regular income, then save to cover it.

- Keep saving after birth-childcare costs add up fast!

We seemed to 'need' so many things for the baby. I set about working out how to buy everything as cheaply as possible. My first piece of advice is to buy as much as you can second-hand. We went to "Little Pickles" Markets and car boot sales. Even though I was trying to keep it cheap, we still bought way too much stuff.

PAYING THE ADHD TAX

I've paid 'ADHD tax' all my life, and when I was pregnant, there was no exception. When I was about seven months pregnant, we went down to Devon to see James' mum for a few days. I was really excited about having a break from work.

It was a 4.5-hour drive to Bratton Clovelly, which was uncomfortable, and by the time we got there, all I wanted to do was put my PJs on and get into bed. James went to get my bag from the car, then he reappeared, empty handed.

'What bag did you bring?' he asked me.

'The suitcase with the owls on it', I replied. James' face dropped and that was when I knew I had nothing with me except the clothes on my back. I had forgotten to put my bag in the car.

What a catastrophuk*!

We were staying for a week, and it was time to pay my ADHD tax. This is a real thing – typically someone with ADHD spends around £1,600 a year more than someone who is neurotypical, which is all because the way our brains function on an executive level makes us forgetful.[2]

That doesn't just mean we forget things like our suitcase when we travel – we might forget to read the small print, forget to pay for a parking ticket or forget to cancel subscriptions. We can also forget to make payments on time, which means we incur late fees, and we can end up buying things we already have or impulse shopping – sound familiar?

At seven months pregnant, ADHD tax this time meant driving to Exeter to buy clothes, which I knew I would only wear for about another six weeks. Having to spend money on these kinds of things made me rage. Since getting out of debt I'd been super careful with my money.

I was making rational decisions when I was shopping, and always asked myself if I needed it or wanted it? Was it going to improve my life? I would keep items in my online cart for 48 hours to make sure I really wanted them.

---

[2] *Living with ADHD can cost an extra £1600 a year because of difficulties managing your money* (2022). https://monzo.com/blog/the-extra-costs-of-living-with-adhd

Is It Worth It?

I calculate **cost per wear** before buying clothes. A £50 skirt worn twice costs £25 per wear, but worn four times, it's just £7. The more you wear it, the closer to 'free' it gets — so choose durable pieces!

But now I needed to buy maternity clothes, even though it was a need I had brought on myself. I tried to be sensible and buy items I could resell afterwards — things like maternity jeans and breastfeeding tops or oversized and stretchy stuff I could wear after I gave birth. I felt rubbish spending money on things I couldn't really afford.

It took the shine off our week away and made the trip even more stressful.

Tips to Avoid ADHD Tax

- Keep track of your subscriptions and their end dates.

- Pay things immediately as soon as you open them if you can.

- Don't overcomplicate things.

- Create a simple budget.

- Track your spending.

- Ask for help with small print like T&Cs.

- Use Post-it notes, reminders and alarms to make sure you don't miss bill payments.

- Body-double so that you've got someone to make you pay bills or go through your payments.

A DRUNKEN NIGHT OUT WITH AN UNEXPECTED ENDING

When we got home, I was pooped so I crashed in front of *Grey's Anatomy*, and James went out to the pub, I think to recover from the stress of the trip. After a lot of 'doomscrolling', I realised it was 2.30 am and James wasn't home. I called his mobile and got no answer. About half an hour later, he came crashing in. I wasn't pleased.

I shouted at him for being so late and not answering his phone. Mid-conversation he ran downstairs and came back with a big bag of Hula Hoops. He asked if I was hungry.

'No, I'm not freaking hungry, it's 3 am!' I yelled.

He opened the packet of crisps, grabbed my hands and said, 'Ok then, will you marry me?'

It suddenly dawned on me that the father of my unborn baby was down on one knee proposing to me with a Hula Hoop!

'Are you really proposing to me? As in seriously?'

'Yes, I love you with all my heart. I want you to be my wife.'

He then reached into his pocket and pulled out the real ring! It was beautiful! An actual diamond!

Even though the idea totally terrified me, of course I said yes. I knew he was my person. He always had been, and I knew he always would be. I was going to be someone's wife!!! Fuzz*!

 Gems of Wisdom

- Be kind to yourself whether you're pregnant or experiencing an illness. When you have ADHD, this can be an overwhelming experience.
- ADHD tax is seriously expensive. Become aware of it and find ways to reduce it in your day-to-day life.

Chapter 19

I'm With You

I'm With You *by Avril Lavigne – from her album* Let Go

The lyrics of this song are really depressing – and this summed up how I felt at this point in my life.

I had my final midwife appointment to talk about my birth plan. My plan was to get this baby out as soon as fuzzing* possible!! I was in constant pain, incredibly tired and thought having the baby would make everything better.

I was so wrong.

D-Day arrived. I was 37 + 2, and the doctors wanted to induce me early due to the cholestasis and my pain. I woke up feeling more nervous than I ever had. I arrived at the hospital at 7.30 am, and they gave me the obligatory procedure to make you go into labour.

I was already 2 cm dilated. This will be quick, I thought. Five hours later, all I'd done was watch *Hollyoaks* (a trashy UK soap). They broke my waters at about 9 pm. My non-existent contractions went from minor to off-the-scale horrific within a matter of minutes. I immediately demanded an epidural!

I'm not good with pain at the best of times, but this was like nothing I had ever experienced before. I was hooked up to drips to make labour happen faster. Then the consultant said there was an emergency so I would have to wait for my epidural. It was an agonising 6½-hour wait, with contractions every 30 seconds or so.

I was exhausted by this point, and as soon as it kicked in, I fell asleep. James had to wake me up for contractions so I could push. It was no use though – I couldn't push out a baby when I was this tired. In the end, they pulled him out with a ventouse, which is basically a posh toilet plunger.

Welcome to the world, baby... We had so many names – 'Jack', 'Henry', 'Oliver' – James even suggested 'Hugo'. He didn't look like any of them. All of a sudden, I had a thought. 'What about "Ben"?'

I'd never met a Ben I didn't like. It was a winner for me. To be honest, I think James would have agreed no matter what I suggested, given the hell he'd just seen me go through.

I held baby Ben in my arms, and suddenly and very violently puked all over James' shoes!

We didn't get to have him for long. Ben was jaundiced and had low blood sugar, so they took him off to the neonatal intensive care unit. I slept for two hours and woke up to find it had been all real. I had a baby. A freaking baby. A baby I instantly loved. But a baby who I already felt I didn't deserve.

I didn't feel like I could 'adult' properly, but more than that I didn't feel like myself anymore. That feeling was a combination of the hormones and my ADHD, not that I knew it at the time. I didn't feel like Ben deserved that version of 'me', the one that felt a shadow of my true self.

OUR NEW NORMAL

The next few weeks were a blur. Ben had a tongue tie. He also screamed from the moment he woke up to the moment he went to sleep. It's normal, I told myself.

I was combination feeding – I tried pumping my breast milk, but it just didn't work. Breastfeeding also made me feel physically sick due to my sensory issues. But I did it for nine months because I was scared of what other people would think of me. James was amazing and would give Ben bottle-feeds in between my breastfeeds.

Do You!

I believe you have to do whatever you need to do to get by when it comes to parenting. We all have different circumstances and different lives, DO what works for you and *fluff everyone else.

The pressure to be a good parent made me feel like a failure from day one. But I wasn't a failure, I was neurodivergent.

I was also mourning the loss of my identity as a child-free person. As I've already said, managing change when you have ADHD is difficult. There is an adjustment period where you get used to your new normal. Give yourself permission to feel your loss without judging yourself for it.

It's also important, especially when you become a parent, to accept that you'll feel out of control sometimes. You have to let go of perfectionism and focus on your strengths and on showing yourself some kindness and compassion.

Keep Track of Your Feelings

Journalling can work for some people, but at least talk to someone. Remember, you are YOU, not just a mum.

LOSING MYSELF

Eight weeks after Ben was born, I started to feel what can only be described as weird. I didn't feel like I was bonding with him. What I didn't know was that ADHD is a huge risk factor for postpartum depression and worse. In fact, if you have ADHD, the risk of developing postpartum depression and anxiety is about five times higher than if you're neurotypical.[1]

I started to see things that weren't there. I would be walking in the street, and I would see myself jumping in front of a car or a bus. Or I would be at the top of the stairs, and I would see myself throwing Ben down them. I knew this couldn't be right. Was my sleep deprivation from Ben's screaming and not sleeping more than half an hour at a time getting to me this much?

I told my mum, which turned out to be the best thing I could have done. She booked me in to see a

[1] Nonacs, R. and Nonacs, R. (2024) 'ADHD as a risk factor for postpartum depression and Anxiety – MGH Center for Women's Mental Health', *MGH Center for Women's Mental Health – Perinatal & Reproductive Psychiatry at Mass General Hospital*, 16 May. https://womensmentalhealth.org/posts/adhd-as-a-risk-factor-for-pmad/

psychiatrist. I should probably have been sectioned, but I was worried about telling anyone in case social services took my baby away. It wasn't that I didn't love him. I just wasn't myself.

What I later realised is that not asking for help would probably have meant I reached a point where my baby did have to be taken away from me. Talking about how you're feeling really helps and means you get the support you need.

How to Speak Up When You're Struggling

First, admit you're struggling – it's hard, but find someone who gets it. A friend, partner or fellow parent can help. A mental health professional or charity support (see Resources) can be life-changing, I know mine was.

I went to stay with my mum for a bit. She basically took Ben and looked after him while I slept. She brought him to me for breastfeeds and not much else. I slept for almost three days straight.

I was never formally diagnosed with postpartum psychosis and the psychiatrist said I had got help just in time. They kept a close eye on me, and I was put on antidepressants. After about four weeks of therapy, I started to feel more like myself.

This was when I started to think about why it had happened. I felt alone, but I was also terrified of being judged. My therapist suggested that I try to make some mum friends. But this felt like my worst nightmare. I was an oversharer by nature, and I was worried I'd walk into the room and tell everyone something really inappropriate like, 'I tried to kill my baby'.

But my therapist insisted. She even found me a baby group in Southampton – Southampton Newbies – that I could attend. The first time I went, I sat in the car and didn't go in. The second time I made it to the end of the road. Third time lucky.

The women in the group were so welcoming that I instantly felt like I had met my people. It was not what I'd expected. I had expected judgy mums, but I found mums who swore, who liked a glass of wine as soon as their baby went to bed and who understood what I was going through. It turned out Ben had a compressed neck muscle, which was quickly sorted with some cranial osteopathy! And things started to get better.

- **Talk about it:** If you're struggling during or after pregnancy, don't brush it off – speak to someone. ADHD brains can spiral, and getting support *can* save your life.

- **Rest isn't optional:** If someone can take the baby while you reset, **let them**. Your brain needs downtime to function.

- **Parent your way:** Co-sleep, bottle-feed, do what works – just follow safety guidelines and ignore the guilt-trippers.

- **Laugh it out:** ADHD brains thrive on humour – funny parenting TikToks can be a lifeline when chaos hits.

Chapter 20

Heartbeats

> **Heartbeats** *by José González – from his album* Veneer
>
> This is the song that James and I walked down the aisle to at our wedding. We chose it because it's all about hope and certainty. With him, I felt a lot more certain about my future.

After five months, I had to go back to work, which was hard. I wasn't ready at all. I wanted to work three days a week, so my boss told me I couldn't go back to my old job as it was full time. Instead, they created a job for me, which also came with a much-needed pay rise.

I became the change management manager. Seriously, what even is that? It seemed to be anything they wanted to throw at me. Training, e-learning, spread-sheets, project management, employee benefits and onboarding. Every day was different; it was the least repetitive job I think I have ever had.

On the plus side, I was never bored. But I would feel really anxious, and I was constantly getting imposter syndrome. I wasn't trained in any of the things I was doing and had to teach myself. But I loved learning and did courses in mentoring, management, sales and coaching – all of which came in handy down the line.

I made sure I didn't work Tuesdays so I could still go to the Newbies group. I loved new parents joining because I felt like I knew more than them and could help them. This was how I discovered that one of my core values is helping others.

I had so much work to do that after about three months, I upped my days to four a week. I didn't want to but I was struggling to get everything done. My boss said she knew how much I was struggling and offered me a work coach. My instant mental reaction was, 'Ugh someone telling me what to do'. I think that was my pathological demand avoidance talking. Then I panicked that they thought I wasn't good at my job.

I was uncomfortable to start with, but after a couple of sessions I was sold. My work coach Jerome was amazing. He made me see that I had potential. In the first session, he pointed me towards a video by a chap named Simon Sinek, 'Why'. I later learned that this is the third most watched TEDx Talk of all time.

In this talk, Simon says, 'People don't buy what you do; they buy why you do it'.[1]

It didn't make much sense to me at the time, and it didn't feel like it related to my job. But I put it to one side to come back to later.

Jerome coached me for months, and I started to actually embrace the job. I made suggestions of how things could be done faster. I played to my strengths and asked for help on the stuff I was struggling with. For the first time ever, I actually liked my job.

I liked the people, I liked the job, I even liked my scary manager. What I realised is that she wasn't scary; she was just very direct. People with ADHD often struggle with this because it triggers our rejection sensitivity dysphoria (RSD). But when I swallowed my pride and accepted the help she offered, it made a world of difference to me.

Accepting Feedback

One of the most powerful things you can do in life is accept feedback. I use the phrase 'I value your feedback. I take it onboard, and I grow'. to help calm my RSD when someone gives me feedback that I find triggering. Feedback is the key to improving in any area of your life, and asking for feedback is the best way to learn.

---

[1] Sinek, S. (Sept. 2009) *How great leaders inspire action.* https://www.ted.com/talks/simon_sinek_how_great_leaders_inspire_action?subtitle=en

My boss saw my potential and did everything she could to help me realise it. I started to get noticed by those in upper management, and I became part of more senior conversations. I felt like I had a purpose, and I was doing really well. My boss put me forward for an award, and I won it!

I was now an award-winning employee. All thanks to my boss and my amazing coach.

Looking back, I think my boss may have known I was neurodivergent. Of course, she couldn't diagnose me, but she knew she could help in other ways, and for that I was incredibly grateful. She was the first boss I had ever had who truly supported me to get the best out of myself. She made my time employed there really enjoyable for the main part.

James and I had the most gorgeous on a budget wedding, you can read more about that in a blog I wrote recently for Mad About Money app, We didn't have our honeymoon immediately as we needed to plan with a 10-month-old baby. Thanks to our friends' generosity, we were able to book an all-inclusive family holiday to Gran Canaria.

It almost immediately turned into a nightmare. On day two, we all got food poisoning. It was horrific. We only had one toilet between us, and we had to deal with a very poorly baby. Ben got so sick we had to take him to hospital, where they gave him extra fluids and some electrolytes. Five of our seven days away were spent doing the high-speed bathroom shuffle* and vomiting like something from *The Exorcist*. It wasn't pretty.

Turns out most of the hotel guests got sick. We tried to get our money back, but nothing ever came of it. Luckily the hospital bill was covered by our holiday insurance. Our honeymoon sucked.

I tried to complain but got nowhere. People who have ADHD have a massive sense of justice. It's called 'ADHD justice sensitivity', and it means we have a heightened emotional reaction when things are perceived as unfair, unequal or unjust. Often, this leads to impulsive reactions.

When you have ADHD, you can also shy away from conflict, which makes you less likely to complain. It's another way in which you pay the ADHD tax, because you leave money on the table by not getting refunds when you deserve them.

Helen Dewdney has written a book called ***How to Complain***[2] that has brilliant tips in it about how to get what you're owed when things go wrong. I strongly recommend you read it.

CASE STUDY: WHEN COMPLAINING WORKS

Sam Milburn, Founder of **Could It Be ADHD** Podcast, shared a personal story about an Airbnb booking that

---

[2] Dewdney, H. (2019) *How to Complain: The Essential Consumer Guide to Getting Refunds, Redress and Results!*, 3rd edition.

went wrong with me – it really resonated when
I heard it!

I was massively disappointed when the outside
area of our Airbnb was totally dilapidated.
It was covered in bird poop. There were rusty
chairs, and all the windows and doors were
filthy outside.

We always chose somewhere with an outside
space as my son is autistic and going out for
dinner isn't always an option.

I had booked the house, so I felt an intense
degree of responsibility when things didn't work
out. I thought, 'I should have researched better'
But all the reviews were good, and it was adver-
tised as having a patio space. The outside area
wasn't the only problem. I also had to clean
when we got there. I've got sensory issues and
find it hard to stay somewhere I know hundreds
of people have been. So, when sides are covered in dust, I start overthinking about what
else isn't clean.

My mind at this point was in overdrive. My
impulsivity made me start drafting a message,
which was emotionally driven. But my partner
told me to leave it for today, go for a walk and
message in a few days.

I had the biggest ball of anxiety in my stomach
from the out of control feeling of not knowing
what was going to happen about the complaint
or how the host would react. Would he be

kind or defensive? Needing to have it all fixed now is often too much for me and can lead to panic attacks. So I walked on the beach, took deep breaths, and tried to think about the other lovely things we were going to do that week.

Later that evening I redrafted my complaint into a very factual response. The next day it turned out there was no hot water, and the boiler was broken. I still hadn't raised the complaint, so I was feeling very anxious.

The owner refunded us £171 for the inconvenience of no hot water for 30 hours or so and was very helpful. This made it easier for me to lead in with the other complaints. On the last day I told the owner he seemed like a great person and perhaps others had never raised issues about the cleaning and unusable outdoor space (he wasn't local). I sent pictures and asked for a refund of the same again. He paid it with no question.

I don't like complaining as my mind goes into overdrive anticipating what the response might be. It's like there are a thousand ways it could go, and my brain tries to anticipate them all, so that I can prepare a response for all eventualities. Until it's resolved I'll feel anxious and sick.

So yes, it's easier not to complain. But I try to look at the situation as if I was on the other side. I'd want to know. I'd want the opportunity to put it right. I try to hold onto the thought that most people are nice. My sense of injustice is also something that will propel me into getting to the bottom of it and override the anxiety.

Sam's story shows how important it is to avoid acting impulsively. The irony is, if you complain from an emotionally driven place, you're more likely to cause upset to the other person, which will make it less likely that you'll receive a refund.

- **Put it in writing:** email leaves a paper trail. If needed, find the CEO's contact at ceoemail.com.

- **Stay polite:** customer service reps aren't the enemy; politeness gets better results.

- **Stick to facts:** avoid accusations; use neutral language like *'it appeared to me that. . .'.*

- **Be clear and concise:** use bullet points, dates and reference numbers; include photos if relevant.

- **Know your rights:** The Consumer Rights Act 2015 protects your purchases and services.

- **State what you want:** be clear on whether you seek a refund, repair or apology.

- **Set a deadline:** give them a time frame to respond before escalating.

- **Follow through:** if ignored, be ready to escalate to the Ombudsman, Trading Standards or Small Claims Court.

Here are some additional tips that I find helpful for complaining as an ADHDer:

- Pause before reacting. Take a breath to help you resist being impulsive or having an emotional outburst.

- Give yourself time to think things through before responding.

- Get clear about what you're complaining about. Write it down and prioritise the issues that are bothering you the most.

- Avoid making vague statements like 'everything is wrong'. Be specific and offer solutions such as, 'Could you replace this product?' or 'Could you issue a refund?'

- Use neutral phrases like, 'I'm disappointed with. . .' or 'I'm frustrated by. . .' and try to avoid going off topic.

🔷 Gems of Wisdom

- Feedback can trigger our RSD, but it will help you develop in all areas of your life. Learn how to manage your response so that you don't take it personally and see it as a learning opportunity.

- Budgeting helps with more than just getting you out of debt. Apply those skills to things like wedding planning.

- Don't be scared to complain and don't take the response to your complaint personally. It often feels hard, but it's worth it to not leave money on the table.

Chapter 21

Go Your Own Way

> **Go Your Own Way** *by Fleetwood Mac – from their album* **Rumours**
>
> This is one of my dad's favourite songs. Hearing it on a night out at a point when I had no direction prompted me to go my own way and start my business.

When I came back to work after our honeymoon, everything was odd. Management were having lots of meetings, and for some reason, I wasn't being invited. I started panicking that I had done something wrong again.

The next day we all got called into the boardroom.

'We have bad news...'

We had lost the account we were all working on, and we had two choices. Switch to the new company taking it over or get made redundant.

It came as a big shock. I loved my job, and I couldn't face the idea of having to look for another one.

Luckily, they gave us a lot of warning. It was November and the contract wasn't ending until March. This was the first employer I had ever had who I felt valued me, and I had to leave. I was so sad. Once again, I was faced with working out what the hell I was going to do with my life.

What to Do If You Discover You're Being Made Redundant

- **Don't panic:** Take time to take stock of the situation and emotionally process before making your next move. Work out how much redundancy money you'll receive and how long it will last.

- **Don't take it personally:** Your rejection sensitivity dysphoria (RSD) will kick in, but it's not your fault. Focus on how to make the best of the situation.

- **Give yourself permission to feel all your emotions:** Talking to a trusted friend or therapist about how you're feeling can help reduce overwhelm.

- **Get references from your employer:** Especially LinkedIn recommendations.

- **Start thinking about what you want to do next:** Lean into your strengths and look for roles that align with your values and passions.

- **Look for neurodivergent-friendly employers:** See if they have a disability and inclusivity statement on their website. Ask in interviews how they'll support your neurodivergent condition.

- **Prioritise self-care:** Our ADHD brains can hyper-focus on problems, so we need to make sure we're eating well and still doing the things we enjoy. This will help reduce stress.

FINDING MY PURPOSE

After I had Ben, I set up a parenting forum on Facebook to support other parents with their mental health and it had been growing steadily. It was my first taste of running a community. Could I make money from that somehow?

Then I remembered a hairbrained idea I'd had a few months earlier about how I could help parents to save money on things they bought regularly. I started to wonder if I could be self-employed again. I knew I was going to get redundancy money. I could use that to start a business.

But then my negative thoughts kicked in. I had been bad at running a business before! I wasn't a good business owner. Although I now realised I hated recruitment, so maybe this would be different. Helping other people really aligned with my values, and this was something I was really passionate about and could put my personality into. It also brought my life experience into business.

I had a while to think about it, but I started to save money.

The more I thought about it, the more I realised I'd learnt valuable lessons from what happened with Purple Cat Recruitment. I could do this.

I started to reach out to local businesses – cafes, soft plays, toy stores and trampoline parks – in Southampton. I had built this amazing community, and I knew if I could help people to save money, they would support me. I had even become sort of a local celebrity and would often get asked if I was 'Maddy from the parenting forum' at kids parties. I always felt simultaneously super uncomfortable and really proud of what I'd created.

My parenting forum had 3,500 members who all lived in Southampton and went to the same places as me with their kids.

I decided I would create a discount card that helped people to shop locally, and I started asking businesses if they would offer discounts to parents in my forum. At this point, I didn't know how successful it would become.

I decided to tell my boss about my plan. She told me that as long as it wasn't affecting my work, she had no problem with me starting the business. Whether you would choose to tell your boss is down to your relationship and how you think they'll take it. If you think your boss will view it as negatively affecting your work, perhaps keep it to yourself, but it's a judgement call you need to make.

Plan for the Conversation

If you decide to tell your boss about your side business, take some time to plan what you're going to say and think about any objections they might have so you can overcome them.

All I had to do now was start. I designed a card and paid £350 to print the cards. I launched on 1 December, and I sold 70 cards at £19.99–£1,399.30 in my first month of business. I didn't even have a website. All I had was a Facebook group and a PayPal link!

I was still being paid at this point, so I invested what I'd made so far into printing more cards and making a basic website at low cost. I also got a friend's husband to design a logo.

And I started to talk about it more. I grew the number of businesses who were advertising on the card. I expanded to offer services like plumbers, estate agents and beauty salons. It started to really take off. In my second month, I sold another 150 cards giving me just under £3,000.

My corporate salary after tax was about that, which made me feel confident leaving my job with three months of redundancy money. The next few months passed in a bit of a blur.

I had soon sold over 400 cards; people were loving it. I called it the 'My VIP Card', with 'VIP' standing for 'Very Important Parent'. I became known as the 'VIP lady'. I knew it wasn't going to be easy, but I could totally do this.

FROM STRENGTH TO STRENGTH

I spoke to James, who said I had three months to make it work. That was in 2017. I haven't worked for anyone else since – apart from a couple of temp jobs when there was too much month and not enough money.

Running a business isn't for the faint hearted, but it's great for ADHD-ers *if* you plan and know what you're selling and who you're selling it to. Use everything you've learnt about planning in other areas of your life (and the tips I've already shared) and apply this to business.

I went back to networking. I hated it after my previous experiences, but I knew I needed to spread the word to more people if I was going to grow. I'd psych myself up in the car before I went in. I worried about saying the wrong thing, or people not taking me seriously. No one ever realised how nervous I was. They all thought I was super confident.

Getting Yourself Out There

You don't have to pay to go to pure networking events – in fact, in my experience, these are often a bit of a waste of money. Instead, you can go to other events where you learn something, but there are still other people in the room. That way, there's less pressure to network and 'sell'. Instead, it's more conversational and much easier, especially if you're nervous about the idea of networking.

Networking in some shape or form is important for building any business, but you can think outside the box and still make valuable connections without having to sign up to every business networking event going.

But people did take me seriously! Someone from the **Daily Echo** newspaper in Southampton was at one of the meetings, and I got my first-ever bit of newspaper coverage. It had the worst headline ever!

'Mum was afraid she was going to kill her baby.'[1]

This headline made me out to be some sort of child killer! That wasn't me and I didn't try to kill my baby! It put me off looking for any more PR for a while.

---

[1] Staff, D.E. (2018) 'Mum was afraid she was going to kill her baby', *Daily Echo*, 29 March. https://www.dailyecho.co.uk/news/15653798.mum-afraid-going-kill-baby/

It did, however, help me to gain another thousand members in my parenting forum! I was happy to have more people to sell to and help, but that article triggered my RSD.

I was making good money, around £3,000–£4,000 most months. I found an accountant, and as I was terrible at the admin side of running the business, I also found a virtual assistant, Katie. I loved her. She was so helpful. She would process payments and keep track of my spending and finances.

By this point, my personal finances were in a good place. I wasn't struggling anymore. Not only was I managing to pay myself, but I was also putting money into growing the business.

I learnt how to market myself on social media by following experts and learning from the gurus. I posted every day. I networked at least twice a week. I started to get contacted by businesses in neighbouring cities – Winchester, Portsmouth and Bournemouth – so I started to expand.

In hindsight, I think I expanded too quickly. The business became all-consuming and felt overwhelming at times. But it was making me money. I met someone at a networking meeting who said that they knew someone who did employee benefits and that I should target employers. Working in my last job, I had learned a lot about employee engagement and benefits. Maybe I could do this.

I had a LinkedIn account from years ago. After about 75 attempts to reset my password, I got in and updated my profile. I created a page, so it showed on my profile and shared my first post.

I had no idea what I was doing. I posted that I had started a business and that I was helping parents to save money and support small businesses. People started to connect with me. It was crazy!

I fumbled my way through social media. I had never had an Instagram account, so I created one. I made a Facebook page, in addition to the forum, and I started to post a couple of times a day.

I joined a new networking business, Hampshire Women's Business, and started to make some business friends there. I remember thinking I had found my people when they randomly burst into song at the first meeting I went to. It was mainly mums and other people who were fairly new to business, just like me.

Everyone was really accepting. Trudy Simmons, who ran it, was about as mad as they come but she had an energy of pure drive and support. It was all about community with her and I knew I could learn a lot from this lady. She was a great role model – positive but realistic.

Tips for Growing an Audience to Sell To

- Work out who your audience is. If you try to sell to everyone, you'll end up selling to no one.

(continued)

- Learn which platforms your ideal clients will hang out on and go there. You don't need to be on every platform.

- Be consistent. Don't give up before you've started. Growing an audience takes time.

- *TikTok* has been game changing for me.

I hadn't stepped much outside of the parenting forum for sales, but I knew I needed to be more visible. Then, Trudy announced that she was running the Hampshire Women's Business Awards.

I entered a couple of categories: 'Phenomenal Product' and 'Hampshire Women's Business of the Year'. Not long after, I found out I was a finalist for both! I was so shocked that, after just a year, my business was up for two awards.

 Gems of Wisdom

- If you face an unexpected change, like redundancy, give yourself time and space to process your emotions and to think about what you want to do next. Could this be a chance to try something new?

- If you set up your own business, play to your strengths. Use your ADHD to your advantage and get help for the areas (like admin and accounting) if you struggle with those areas.

- Use social media to build a following. It's free and a great way to grow an engaged community who will support your business.

Chapter 22

Drunken Lullabies

> **Drunken Lullabies *by Flogging Molly – from their album* Drunken Lullabies**
>
> Around this time, I started to unravel, so I started drinking more and going out more. At the time I thought it was helping, but really it was hindering.

Shortly after the award nominations, one of my old university mates invited me to Barcelona for her hen do. I suddenly realised that I hadn't had a day off since starting the business and said yes instantly. It felt good to say yes after years of scrimping and saving.

Not taking time off is a common challenge for ADHD-ers who run businesses. We get caught up in what we're doing and focus on nothing else. Society tells us we have to 'hustle', and we do. But what I've realised is that we don't have to hustle all the time.

Remember Why You Started in Business

Learn what you need from your business to make **you** happy. Write down your values and what's important to you. Remind yourself why you became self-employed in the first place. When you clarify what you're doing and why, you'll be more success-ful than if you just wing it.

GETTING AWAY

James and I have always co-parented, and he was very supportive about me going away for a few days. I was really looking forward to it – even though I hate flying. I find the loss of control scary, and if we hit turbu-lence, from a sensory perspective, it's just awful. The only thing that helps is reminding myself of the actual statistics around the safety of flying.

Despite hating the plane, I loved it as soon as we arrived in Barcelona. We had a gorgeous villa, and it was great to be with my uni mates – Beth, Zoe and Kath – again. We partied for three days straight – clubbing, cocktails, even an ice bar.

While we were there, I'd promised Zoe I'd walk to the Sagrada Familia with her. It was a long walk; it was hot and I'm totally unfit. I was also hungover and hadn't taken any water with me. When we reached the cathedral, I felt really woozy and had to sit on a bench. All of a sudden, I puked in a bush.

I took a taxi back to our villa and had a nap. That night I still didn't feel right, so I didn't drink with dinner. Plus, we had a late flight home, and I knew I had to drive once I got back. I slept for a couple of hours on the flight and thought I'd be fine to drive. Plus, I'd never understood how anyone could fall asleep at the wheel... Until it happened to me.

I caught myself drifting into the middle lane; my eyes wanted to close so badly. What was wrong with me? I pulled over at the next service station and slept for three hours. After that, I felt a lot better, although I still had to pull over four more times to pee on the drive home.

ROUND TWO...

I had Sunday to spend with Ben and James, but Monday was manic. I was still really tired and felt like I needed another holiday to get over Barcelona. I was booked for a networking event that evening, but as soon as I drove off, the seatbelt gave me a squeeze – ouch! Why are my boobs so sore? I thought.

I pulled over and called Rosie, one of my closest mum friends. We spent so much time together that our periods had synced. 'Hey Rosie, erm, when is your period due?' I asked. 'It was last week, why?' she replied...No freaking way*! Here we go again!

I drove straight to Sainsbury's and made a beeline for the pregnancy test aisle. I grabbed a Clear Blue, paid for it and went straight to the toilets. I peed on the stick. I waited... Pregnant 3–4. Mother Hubbard*!

Then I started worrying. Barcelona was so messy that I was pretty sure I'd given my baby foetal alcoholism. I walked out of the supermarket in a daze. The venue for networking was nearby, so I walked in a few minutes late and in true ADHD fashion announced that I was pregnant to the whole room and then burst into tears.

I was happy, as we'd been trying for a while, but it felt overwhelming. Then I realised I'd told a room full of strangers I was pregnant before I'd told my husband. I had another test in the box, so I decided I'd take that one at home, with James, and pretend I didn't know.

I got home. I did the test... Not pregnant. WTF?! How was that possible? Maybe it was just a false alarm, but it explained so much. I couldn't tell James I'd already taken a test that said I was pregnant, and I couldn't face going out to buy more, so I waited until the morning. I took two more tests – both said 'Pregnant'.

James was shocked, but happy. Two kids. Then, my internal monologue started again... But I can barely cope with one. What am I going to do about the business?

As the weeks went on, I felt worse and worse. The sickness was worse this time. I was constantly vomiting. It got in the way of things I enjoyed. Yet again, I was miserable. At seven weeks, they tested me for gestational diabetes, and of course, it was another piece of fruit*! Just my luck. I felt like I wasn't very good at having babies.

Ben was excited; he was going to have a baby brother or sister. He would stroke my tummy and say, 'Hi baby', which was super cute.

When I was 15 weeks pregnant, we went to Butlin's for a week. I already had a bump the size of a watermelon. I was still feeling sick, and the food at the buffet made me feel worse. The bed was like sleeping on a plank of wood. At least swimming helped me take the weight off my bump, and Ben loved it, especially going on the trampolines.

After a week, I was very ready to go home, but our car had other ideas. The battery had died, and we had to wait a day for a tow truck. I was getting worried about not working and realised that I was terrible at taking time off.

HOW TO TAKE MORE TIME OFF

I've since come to understand the benefits of having a semi-passive income. This means you create an asset that you can sell multiple times, or you build a community that people pay to join. There are lots of opportunities to create a passive income in most businesses – I wish I'd thought of some of these before I got pregnant again.

- Create an online course.

- Create digital downloads that people can pay to access.

- Build a paid membership community where you give tips and advice. This is less passive, as you still have to be involved, but it will give you a recurring income.

Having a membership community also gives you a group of engaged people who are more likely to want to pay to come to your events or take masterclasses with you. You can even run exclusive events for them, for an additional fee. This is a huge topic – one for my next book!

 Gems of Wisdom

- Take time off. You will regret it if you don't and you're highly likely to burn out if you work every hour of the day. This is true whether or not you're having a baby by the way!

- Explore opportunities for passive income. This would have helped me take more time off as maternity leave if I'd thought about it sooner.

Chapter 23

Everybody Wants to Rule the World

Everybody Wants to Rule the World
by Tears for Fears – from their album
Songs from the Big Chair

This was one of my favourite songs when I was little. I remember listening to it in the car with my parents – now my kids love it too! My business felt like it was on the up and I felt like I was going to take over the world.

Even though I was feeling awful due to my pregnancy, the business was doing really well. I had over 600 businesses offering a discount to my members, and I had nearly 2,000 paying customers. I decided to branch out. I already had a diverse range of discounts in Hampshire, Dorset and Wiltshire. Was it time to try and conquer the UK?

I thought so! Until I realised that someone local had ripped off my business model! She had started to message all of my businesses and tell them her discount card was better. Most of them weren't buying what she was selling.

I reached out to her and offered her a job – if she was good at sales, maybe I could get her working with me instead of against me? We met for coffee and got on really well. She had a lot of drive and determination, which I really liked. She gave me the idea of having territory managers for different areas, who are paid a basic and a commission. She ended up screwing me over, she was just fishing for info.

I focused on the corporate side of my business because I could get more money that way. The Hampshire Women's Business Awards was just two days away, and I knew that networking with the 200 people in that room would also boost my visibility.

The night before the awards I went out for dinner with the girls, whom I hadn't seen in ages. We went to a local Greek restaurant, where I ordered halloumi fries, king prawns and some feta and olives. It was a lovely evening, but on the way home I started to feel really unwell.

By the time I got home, I was struggling to breathe, and I was covered head to toe in hives. It looked like I had been rolling around in a bunch of stinging nettles! Luckily, the breathing difficulties didn't last long. We called 111, and they said I was likely having an allergic reaction to the prawns.

I knew that I was allergic to shellfish but not prawns – and I love prawns! Apparently, you become more sensitive to these things when you're pregnant. Thankfully, the allergy didn't last after I had the baby.

I was so itchy and worried about my breathing that I didn't sleep that night. The next morning, I decided I couldn't go to the awards ceremony. I called Trudy to let her know. She was insistent that I go. 'You *have* to come!', she said. 'Get some sleep now and be here later'.

My first thought was, maybe I've won something! Then I talked myself out of it – of course I hadn't, my business had only been going for a year. But thanks to Trudy's insistence, I rested and got myself ready for the ceremony that evening.

I arrived at the awards and sat with one of my favourite networking friends, Bridget. As the night went on, I increasingly felt that Trudy had wanted me there to make up the numbers. But I made the most of networking, including meeting a franchising expert who told me I should consider that for my business. I decided that was an option for the future.

Before I knew it, they were announcing one of the two categories I was nominated in: Phenomenal Product. As they read out the nominees, I was practising my 'gracious loser' face.

And the winner is... Maddy Alexander-Grout!

What?! I had won! I was an award-winning business owner! I was so overwhelmed that I burst into tears. My acceptance speech was basically me thanking Katie, my VA, for being awesome on steroids. I couldn't believe that my little business that I started from my sofa had won an award!

I barely listened to the rest of the awards. They all blurred into each other. I'm usually really supportive of other people, but I was so tired and now I was also feeling happy and emotional.

'And now for Hampshire Women's Business of the Year...' Trudy said from the stage.

I knew I was nominated, but I was sure I had fuzzled up the interview. I had overshared so badly, talking about my postpartum psychosis and how I'd struggled with starting a business. I wasn't even practising my sore loser face, since I knew I hadn't won it.

And the winner of Hampshire Women's Business of the Year goes to...

Maddy Alexander-Grout!!

What the fresh merry hell*?! They said my name, and I froze to the spot. 'Maddy it's you!!!!' Bridget said. I gave the biggest cheesy smile, and burst into tears! I couldn't believe it. I was the best woman in business in my county!

In one night, I went from having no awards to being a multi-award-winning business owner. After I had recovered, the first thing I did was share the news everywhere! I contacted the local paper and the local radio station and managed to get interviews for both. I shared far and wide on social media, tagging the sponsors and Trudy in my posts.

I contacted local podcasters and asked to go on their podcasts. I talked to literally everyone about it. It can seem really self-indulgent to big yourself up, but it is so important. If you win something, you need to shout about it because you need the visibility.

RIDING THE WAVE

After winning the awards, more businesses than ever contacted me to join the programme. I had window stickers printed so business owners could show they were part of the scheme. I added national discounts where people could buy vouchers and get cashback into an account. The card was growing in popularity every day.

My social media was growing, my reach was growing and friends were telling their friends. I sponsored events to get in front of corporates and attended business shows and exhibitions. I pushed myself out there every single day. I had a motto which I still have to this day.

'Do one thing every day that pushes you forward'.

This reflects my life, not just my business. We all need to develop our resilience, so we can push through the tough times, but we also need to know when it's time to let something go.

Life can be really rough, if I have learned anything from my life is that life gives you lemons. And when it does, add some gin and get over it.

Tips for Building Resilience

- Develop a PFMA (positive fu*king mental attitude). It sounds cliché, but if you think good things, then good things will happen, and fu*king gives it FORCE!

- Get good people around you and put some distance between yourself and anyone toxic – or better yet remove them from your life completely.

- Look after your mental health. You can't pour from an empty cup, or even a half-full one.

- Don't fear failure and don't fear success both come with positives and learnings.

(continued)

- Set goals for your life and your business. I use the FART method: *FABULOUS* – Do things that give you joy and fill your cup, things that bring you joy bring you success. *AUTHENTIC* – Always be you, the real you will attract what you need from the universe. *REACHABLE* – Make sure that you are not aiming too high; whilst it's great to aim high, do it in little chunks. Success doesn't have to be fast or overnight. *TRACKABLE* – Make sure you can track and give yourself little rewards.

- Focus on your passions. If you don't love what you do, then you'll get bored and lose momentum. This is especially important if you have ADHD.

HOW TO NAIL GOAL SETTING (WITHOUT GIVING UP AND WITHOUT BEATING YOURSELF UP)

Goal setting, and following through on your goals, can be particularly tricky if you have ADHD. Linda Scerri, business and storytelling strategist from `lindascerri.com`, has shared these five tips to help you nail goal setting:

1. **Write it down:** you're more likely to achieve a goal if it's on paper (or screen).

2. **Break it up:** small steps make big goals less overwhelming.

3. **Ditch the to-do list:** use sticky notes, an app, or set goals as your screensaver.

4. **Celebrate wins:** tick off progress and give your-self a dopamine boost.

5. **Stay flexible:** adjust as needed; progress beats perfection.

Checking in on what's going on in your business and your world is really important. Keep asking yourself if your business is bringing you joy, whether you have the time you want to spend with your family and whether it's making enough money for you. You need to constantly evaluate your goals based on where you are in your journey.

One of the best ways I've found to assess this is by working out my return on my investment in my busi-ness: am I getting back as much, if not more, time, energy and money than I'm putting in? If the answer is no, this might be a sign that it's time for a change, presuming you've given your business enough time in the first place.

If you're an ADHD-er like me, it's easy to make impul-sive decisions. When it comes to business, you don't want to throw the baby out with the bathwater, but you also don't want to flog a dead horse. Get some help from a coach or mentor who can help you see where you need to focus your efforts and who can help regulate the hundreds of ideas you'll have for your business.

Let's be honest, us ADHD-ers are idea factories, but not all of our ideas will be good. I've had millions of terrible ideas. Someone outside of your thought process can help you sort the good from the bad and downright awful ideas.

Gems of Wisdom

- Focus on what you're doing and don't let other people who might copy you get to you. There's room for everyone and, in some cases, you might even be able to work together for everyone's benefit.

- Shout about your achievements. The more visible you become, the more your business will grow.

- Set goals and get help to keep you on track if you need it. If you need some accountability, try tactics like body doubling and batching tasks.

Chapter 24

Believer

Believer *by Imagine Dragons – from their* album Evolve

I actually hate this song, but it's Harriet's hyper-focus and she makes me put it on in the car all the time. In fairness, this song also talks about transformation, personal growth, self-acceptance, hope and resilience, which is all pretty apt for this stage of my life.

The next few weeks brought me a hell of a lot of lemons, and I couldn't even drink gin! My pregnancy went from bad to worse. Our baby, a girl, was being a monkey. She was rolling over a nerve in my tummy; I was in agony all the time, and in and out of hospital. Three weeks before my scheduled induction, they decided to admit me.

I was frustrated. I had so much work to do, and I wasn't planning on having much time off.

I was convinced that I wasn't going to make it to my induction day, and that she was going to come early, but she was stubborn.

Ben and James came to see me a lot. I just wanted to be home. The weekend before she came, they let me out – but only on day release! It was like I was a prisoner. Luckily, the doctors and nurses in Princess Anne Hospital were so nice; I had been in so long that they were becoming friends!

My mum picked me up; I went to her house for a bit and then we took Ben to a play centre with his cousin. I was huge, waddling around like a duck with a stick up my bum. After a lovely morning at the play centre, I went to the pub – not for booze, although it was really tempting.

James collected me from my mum's and took me to another of our locals, The Freemantle Arms, to watch the rugby. England were playing France in the Six Nations, and we kicked their ass – not a regular occurrence, so I took it as a sign of good things to come.

We celebrated our victory and then James took me back to the hospital. I was sad to be back in, but I only had three days until induction day, which fell on Valentine's Day.

> ## Preparing for Labour When You Have ADHD
>
> - Prepare for labour by learning what to expect without over-Googling, making a flexible birth plan, packing your hospital bag early to reduce overwhelm and informing your midwife about your ADHD and any sensory needs.

THE NEW ARRIVAL

It was D-Day.

The first thing I said to the midwife when she came in to get me was '**I want an epidural**!' I thought I would get that in early in case I had to wait. She wheeled me to the delivery suite – Room 3 – the same one I'd given birth to Ben in. I felt so overwhelmed.

It took three midwives and what looked like a massive knitting needle to break my waters. The whole process was really painful. Any dignity I had had left the building!

As soon as my waters broke, the contractions started coming in thick and fast. The anaesthetist came to give me my epidural, which happened so quickly I barely felt it. It wasn't nearly as painful as the one I had with Ben.

The next bit comes with another **massive** trigger warning.

I asked the midwife how long it would take to work. She told me half an hour. What felt like the longest 30 minutes passed, and I could still feel everything.

'Just give it a bit longer Maddy, it will work, don't you worry', she said.

I could feel everything. The contractions were getting closer together by the second.

'It's not working!', I screamed at them.

They got the anaesthetist to come in and check me, 'Hmmm, it doesn't look like it's working, does it?' he said.

'No Sh*t, Sherlock!!', I screamed in a flusterblast*.

He topped the epidural up. I waited another extremely painful half an hour. 'I want something else', I said. I had completely forgotten all my manners by this point.

'No can do', said the midwife, 'You are 7 cm, we can't give you anything for the pain now Maddy, sorry love'.

I had never been in so much pain, my whole body felt consumed. I was sweating like a sumo wrestler in a fight, and I was crushing James' hand, who looked really concerned for me.

About a minute later, I screamed, 'She's coming! I need to push!'

The midwife told me not to as I was still only at 7 cm, but I couldn't control my body. She wanted out and my body was telling me to push, so I pushed. In fact, I pushed her out in one.

I looked down at my baby. She wasn't crying. She was grey and floppy. The cord was wrapped around her neck.

The midwife told James to pull the emergency cord behind him and what felt like a million people rushed into the room and rushed her out of the room.

By this point, I was screaming, 'Where's my baby?! Where's my baby?! Is she dead? Tell me she isn't dead!'

Eight minutes went by. James had to pin me down to the bed, I was hooked up to all sorts of machines and I was losing a lot of blood. They had to give me a lot of stitches. I'm not sure how many exactly but I always tell people it was 42, as it's my lucky number. And who doesn't want a lucky foof?

Then, a midwife appeared, 'She is breathing, she gave us a bit of a scare there, didn't she?' I have never been so relieved about anything in my life.

Another 10 minutes passed and then someone brought me my baby. They'd cleaned her up and she was beautiful. She looked almost identical to Ben.

I couldn't believe what had happened. I was getting stitched up as they handed her to me. 'Chuck an extra couple of stitches in there for me will you', I said (I was only half joking!).

My baby had almost died in front of me, but my body knew she wasn't okay and knew she needed out. It's amazing the miracles our bodies can perform. But she was here.

OUR LITTLE MIRACLE

We named her Harriet. I hadn't researched it, but I really liked the name and felt drawn to it. I later found out it means 'home ruler' – and she really is, I can tell you that much.

They kept us in for a couple of days. It was a similar story to Ben – low blood sugar and she needed a sleep on the baby sunbed for her jaundice.

Ben came in to meet her the day after with James. He was so in love... .

...With the dinosaur I had bought him! 'Mummy, I'm going to call him Stevie!' Ben told me. That was actually another one we'd considered for Harriet after Stevie Nicks. Ben didn't seem too bothered by Harriet, although he did give her a kiss, which was super cute. 'I like baby Harri Mummy', he said. Aww baby Harri – that stuck.

Baby Harri got to come home the next day. I was in love; she was just perfect.

- **Trust your body:** it knows what to do, even if your ADHD brain craves all the info.

- **Plan extra rest:** time blindness means you'll likely need more than you expect.

- **Say yes to help:** decision fatigue and overwhelm will hit, so take support when offered!

Chapter 25

Beating Heart Baby

> **Beating Heart Baby** *by Head Automatica – from their album* Decadence
>
> This is one of my and Rach's favourite songs, but it reminded me of this time because Harri came through her ordeal at birth and her heart started beating.

The first few weeks I coped quite well. Even though I worried in the back of my mind that the psychosis could come back, I had a lot of support. Jenny came to stay for a few days, and my mum was brilliant too. I also had a steady stream of friends offering to help with washing up, cooking and holding Harri while I slept.

James got relegated to the sofa fairly quickly, so that I could safely co-sleep with her. Harri only seemed happy when she had a nipple in her mouth. As you know, I hated breastfeeding, but this time I distracted myself with work and learned how to use social media.

TRUSTING MY GUT

I was contacted by a potential investor. He had heard the business was doing well and wanted to chat. At our meeting, he offered me a large sum of money, but he wanted 50% of the business. Although his ideas to help grow it were very tempting, I didn't feel as though our values aligned.

I had a gut feeling he was a bit of a wheeler dealer, and I could imagine him screwing me over. My business, which I had now been running for three years, was too important to me.

I turned him down. It was hard, because the money he was offering would have been game changing. But something didn't feel right. I trusted my gut, which I don't often do.

ADHD and Professional Boundaries

Saying *no* is hard with ADHD, especially for people pleasers. But setting boundaries earns respect and protects your energy. Don't blur business with friendship, and stop giving too much away— charging is a fair exchange, not a dirty word.

Once I said no, I felt liberated. The potential investor had given me a few ideas. I was still toying with the idea of franchising and I also wanted to run my own awards ceremony: the National VIP Awards.

I started to be more visible than I ever had before, and I took Harri everywhere with me. She was a great ice-breaker at networking events, and a business magnet. I got her a 'My VIP Card' t-shirt, so when she came out with me, she was on brand. I spoke at events with her in my arms and went to awards ceremonies with her. That year, I won a further seven awards.

The business was flying, and my social media profile was improving as I showed the real me. However, having Harri with me brought some challenges. Some people thought that bringing a baby to business events was unprofessional, and I was even turned away from two networking events. I felt ostracised and totally on my own.

That was when I started looking for Facebook groups and found MIB – *Mums in Business International* – run by Leona Burton. I loved her vibe and the community of women supporting women, who valued collabora-tion over competition. By going to their online groups, I grew My VIP Card across the country and had ideas about international expansion.

I had found my people and discovered that I loved online networking. It felt less exhausting than in-person networking, where I would tend to soak up other people's energies as someone with ADHD who is also a strong empath.

My VIP Card was thriving, and every day more businesses were signing up to advertise. My biggest regret is not charging them for the privilege. I felt like they were doing me a favour by offering a discount, BUT they wanted a lot from me and all for free.

I created my own business awards, it was super fun and great for my visibility. But once they were over, I had a huge dopamine lull*. I crashed, hard.

> 💎 **Gems of Wisdom**
>
> - If you're working for yourself, make sure you take lunch breaks, give yourself days off and go on holidays. All of this is essential for avoiding burnout.
> - Get a separate work phone and turn it off when you're not working. Don't always be accessible.
> - If you get overwhelmed, it's OK to adjust your boundaries. The key is to openly communicate and be honest with your clients about your ADHD, parenting needs or whatever is impacting your work–life balance.

Chapter 26

Cannonball

Cannonball *by Damian Rice – from his album* **O**

This song is all about releasing things that aren't
serving you. I suffered from PTSD after Harri's
birth, it was the most horrific thing I'd ever
been through.

Burnout. Proper burnout. I regretted not taking some
maternity leave, and I was annoyed with myself for not
saving enough money to support my maternity leave.
Although I'd thought about applying for statutory
maternity pay, it looked like a complete hasslefest*.
I couldn't bring myself to do it. I thought I was stupid
and too lazy to do the forms.

The awards gave me a massive high, followed by a huge low. Planning them had taken all my energy, and my sales had dipped as I'd taken my focus away from selling cards. I was in a hole. I was run down. I felt tired all the time. I was waking up feeling hungover even when I hadn't drunk anything at all. I couldn't get through the day without a nap.

Something had to change. I decided to put Harriet into a nursery. By this point, Ben had started school, which had saved us money. I decided it was time to repurpose it. A quick search of local nurseries told me that this wasn't an option – over £1,500 a month for school hours. No chance I could afford that. Childminders seemed a lot more reasonable, and I found a good option locally who was a cross between a childminder and a nursery. Harri started going there three days a week.

OUT FOR THE COUNT

I was so low that I slept for the rest of December. I totally lost interest in the business. I became withdrawn from social situations, and I felt utterly useless. The fatigue was awful. Harri still wasn't sleeping through the night, even in the bed with me, and James was still on the sofa. I decided to go to the doctor.

'You are depressed Mrs Alexander-Grout. Let's try you on sertraline'.

I took the pills home. I didn't think I was depressed, but I knew I was low. I put it down to utter exhaustion.

I'm not against taking antidepressants at all but this didn't feel like what I needed. Even though my mental health was suffering, I also felt like something physical was going on.

Then, I watched a Davina McCall documentary about menopause (mainly because I love her), which convinced me I was perimenopausal. It took me four weeks to book a follow-up appointment. My blood tests revealed I was showing signs of perimenopause, vitamin D deficient and that there was something up with my thyroid.

My doctor didn't know what the thyroid issue might be, so referred me to the endocrine team at the hospital.

I had to wait about six weeks for my referral appointment. Us ADHD-ers aren't good at waiting – we want answers right now. Of course, I took matters into my own hands and paid 'Dr Google' a visit.

I knew I shouldn't, but I was sick of feeling so fuzzing* awful all the time. I put all of my symptoms into Google. The answer... Hashimoto's disease.

Hashimoto's means that all of the healthy cells in your body attack your thyroid making it underactive. Your body is fighting itself all the time and it's exhausting. And I was also, to top it off, peri menopausal.

I was actually relieved – at least now I knew why I was always so tired. I was prescribed a drug called *levothyroxine*, which was supposed to help me but did jack all!

I was feeling sluggish, tired and unusually ratty. I would go from cool as a cucumber to hot as a jalapeno in less than 10 seconds. The rage was insane, the kids were feeling it, and I was living with permanent mum guilt for how awful I was being to both the kids and James.

I felt so overwhelmed, like I was ready to burst. I'm sure the stress and trauma I'd been experiencing weren't helping, but it was clear that I needed to do something if the drugs weren't working. I had to drastically change my diet, cutting down on booze, sugar and processed foods. All of that made me miserable. I hadn't realised how heavily I still relied on sugar for dopamine.

I also had to start doing more exercise. Walking and dancing were about the only things I could manage. I was aiming for a seven-minute wiggle-jiggle break* every day. That might not sound like much, but it was really beneficial for my mental health.

The doctor also prescribed me Clonidine, which is a beta blocker, and a less well-known non-stimulant ADHD medication. This really took the edge off and helped with my sleep. Of course, I still didn't know I had ADHD.

On top of all of this, my periods were all over the place (sorry if this is TMI, but if you hadn't noticed,

I'm an oversharer). I was having shorter periods (about three days), but they were like an avalanche. Plus, in the days leading up to my period, my mental health got worse, and I felt I had no control over my moods. I was starting to have really dark thoughts like I didn't want to be here anymore, I wanted to burn my business to the ground or just pack my bags and run away. This wasn't just PMS; it was something more.

I started to research period-related conditions on *TikTok* and came across premenstrual dysphoric disorder (PMDD). Often, this co-exists with ADHD, not that I knew that at the time. I went to the doctors and told them I thought I had PMDD, and they agreed.

The PMDD meant I was super snappy at certain times of the month. I was experiencing physical symptoms, like really bad migraines, bloating and amped up period pain. I was struggling to sleep, which was only made worse by my perimenopausal symptoms.

What I've since learnt is that PMDD exacerbates ADHD symptoms because of the fluctuation in hormones and the effect it has on our dopamine receptors. I would get the most horrendous brain fog – as though my head was full of candy floss, sticky and impenetrable. It simultaneously felt like nothing and everything was sticking and it meant for 1–2 weeks every month I really didn't want to be here.

Gems of Wisdom

- **Track your symptoms:** if you suspect conditions like Hashimoto's or PMDD, logging patterns (e.g., with the Flo app) can help you predict flare-ups and plan rest days.

- **See a doctor:** self-diagnosing is tempting, but professional support is key.

- **Advocate for yourself:** if your doctor's advice doesn't feel right, don't hesitate to seek a second opinion.

- **Talk about it:** conditions like these are more common than you think!

Chapter 27

Mountains

Mountains *by Biffy Clyro – from their album*
Only Revolutions

This is mine and Zoe's song. It's all about resilience and inner strength, about standing firm
despite life's ups and downs, it's also about the
power of self-belief.

Given everything I'd been through to grow the business and my new health conditions, it's easy to see
how I reached full-on burnout. I needed time off and a
holiday felt like a brilliant idea. My mum and Chris
said that they'd pay for us to join them in Lanzarote
for a week – I couldn't wait.

This was early 2020, and as I avoid watching the news, I had no idea why my mum asked me to bring some face masks out with us for them. I shoved them in my case and then handed them over without giving it too much thought.

I'd promised James I'd take the whole week off, so when I got home, I had to jump straight back into business mode. But I felt like I needed another holiday – we'd had zero sunshine, so my vitamin D and dopamine levels were still really low.

My mental health still wasn't great, although I was seeing a therapist who was helping me feel less useless. My parenting forum was a great support too, especially as Harriet's refusal to really sleep was affecting my mental health.

Tips for Staying on Top of Your Mental Health When You Have ADHD

Sam Munslow, from Blue Monkey Coaching (bluemonkeycoaching.co.uk), has shared the following tips if you're struggling with your mental health.

- **Honour your rhythms:** Don't force productivity when your brain isn't on board. Rest when needed.

- **Use multiple reminders:** Set alarms for tasks and appointments to reduce stress.

(continued)

- **Be honest:** Share when you're overwhelmed; it helps you and others.

- **Manage phone use:** Use it for reminders but limit doom scrolling. Try screen-free time daily.

- **Find your people:** Connect with ADHD communities for support and belonging – Maddy's Invisible To Influential membership is great!

- **Stop comparisons:** You see others' highlights, not their struggles. Focus on your journey.

- **Hydrate and snack smart:** Drink water and keep healthy snacks handy to boost focus and energy.

STRANGE TIMES

After our holiday, I went to Leicester for the MIB Awards, where I was sponsoring and discussing white-labelling My VIP Card with founder Leona. With their 60,000-strong community, it was a huge visibility boost.

A week later, I was invited to London for an interview with *The Sun Savers Money Channel*. The train was eerily empty, and I hadn't heard about the "mystery virus."

At *The News Building*, I went to shake the host's hand. "We're not doing that anymore – virus risk," she said. I shrugged it off, thinking it was an overreaction.

The interview flew by – money-saving tips, my story, and advice for parents. On my way back, I noticed the sea of face masks. That's when I realised – something big was coming.

💎 Gems of Wisdom

- It's really important to take proper time off. I've said it many times now, but that's because it's essential. Give yourself holidays without work. You'll feel better for it.

- Attend events that can broaden your network and put you in touch with more like-minded people. The MIB Awards were great for this.

- Share what you've learnt through your experiences with others. Often, you'll be amazed at how much you know.

Chapter 28

Blinding Lights

> **Blinding Lights** *by All Time Low – from their album* **Blinding Lights**
>
> This was my pandemic anthem! I spent hours on *TikTok* watching the Blinding Lights dance.

On 23 March 2020, Boris Johnson, the British prime minister, came on the news and told us: 'You must stay in your homes'. 'What a buffoon', I remember think-ing! My opinion only got worse as the weeks went by.

What in the world of wizardry* Boris!! Stay in my home with a five-year-old kid and a one-year-old baby! You have to be joking, mate!!

But he wasn't joking. COVID-19 had spread, and people were dying. It turned out that the people wearing those masks weren't overreacting after all.

I immediately went into a complete panic. I hate being at home, and our house, which I'd bought for James and I, was now a sticky, child-infested hellhole. How was I meant to work from home? I didn't even have a desk or a chair! How was I meant to work, for that matter, with two kids under five?!

More than that, I had to do it on my own as James, a kitchen gardener for a large estate, was classed as a key worker. I love my kids dearly, but I'm not the most maternal person and spending 24/7 with them was not my idea of fun. Of course, Harriet decided to start walking on day one of lockdown, so I needed eyes in the back of my head.

She kept making a beeline for the stairs. By the end of that day, I was knackered. I told myself it wouldn't last long. A few days, maybe a week...

Still, I ordered stair gates for the kids' door and the living room, as our stairs were too wide for a gate. It would have to do.

I found it frustrating to have another step in the process of entering a room. I know it sounds silly, but it was one extra thing to contend with that I could do without. As an outside person, we went for as many walks as we were allowed to. The kids always wanted to go to the park, instead of the field, and it was heartbreaking having to tell them we weren't allowed to go to the park.

My mental health was on the floor. I was barely getting any work done. I would long for nap times just so I could have a couple of hours of quiet time. This was when I started using *TikTok* – I couldn't stop watching the videos of people doing the **Blinding Lights** dance. It felt like this song was keeping the nation going.

I wasn't earning any money. My VIP Card sales had dropped off the edge of a cliff. As you can imagine, a discount card that helps you to shop local when you can't leave the house is pretty much null and void. Life felt overwhelming.

Tips for Dealing with Overwhelm

- **Rest your brain:** Time off prevents overwhelm from spiralling.

- **Work in 25-minute blocks:** Focus, then take a break (a walk helps!).

- **Lie down when overwhelmed:** Being horizontal resets your brain.

- **Go barefoot:** Grounding might sound woo-woo, but it works!

- **Ask for help:** Delegate where you can.

- **Get an ADHD coach:** They make a huge difference (I'm great at this!).

PUSHING THROUGH

I tried to sign on, but the process really overwhelmed me, so I didn't do it. But I still needed money. I found out about a local grant for limited companies, and I took out a bounce-back loan. In hindsight, that wasn't the best decision, as the business already had a £5,000 loan that I'd taken out for the franchising.

The problem was that none of us were really aware of how long the lockdown would last. I kept recruiting franchisees as I very much believed in the product. I had hired Jo, one of my favourite school mums, to help me with the website and admin. I used to walk past her house on our daily walk, just in case she was having a cigarette in her garden, and we could have a brief, socially distanced chat. I was craving human interaction.

Then I hired Nic, who was a crowdfunding specialist. She was brilliant and helped me set up our first crowd funding campaign. We did this to raise money to keep the business afloat – it was along the lines of: 'We need your help. Donate to help My VIP Card carry on'.

Thanks to Nic, it was a huge success, and we raised about £9,000, which was enough to keep the lights on, but we still weren't generating any revenue. The franchisees were getting despondent, and I felt like I was carrying the weight of the world on my shoulders.

I had to stay positive for the franchisees. I still believed that once we were out of lockdown, everything would be better. I knew my business model worked.

CRASHING DOWN

In week three of lockdown, Ben knocked a picture frame off the wall with his feet when he was squirming in his seat, and it smashed. I was worried the glass would cut him, so I passed the glass over the stair gate and went back for the frame. I didn't want to leave the mess, so I decided to climb over the stair gate while holding the frame as I didn't have a spare hand to open it. Who am I kidding?! I was trying to cut a corner because I was doing something mundane, and it backfired!

The next thing I knew, I was on the floor, with the kids standing over me. 'Mummy, are you OK?' Ben asked.

I wasn't fuzzing* OK. I was in a world of pain. The stair gate had given way. I had fallen one way, my arm had gone the other, and I'd knocked myself out. I was in agony, and my arm was dangling as it had been pulled out of its socket.

I tried to stay calm. 'Buddy, can you get mummy's phone, please?' I asked Ben. As he handed it to me, I saw the time – 4.45 pm – James wouldn't be home for another hour. I called him.

Luckily, he'd left work early as they had an order for London, so he was literally around the corner. I needed an ambulance, but I didn't want to call for one as other people needed them more. James said he'd drive me to the hospital, adding, 'First of all, we need to get that arm back in...'

Instant terror surge*. 'You cannot be serious!! You are not popping my arm back in! Not a fuzzing* chance...'

But he popped my arm back in. Apart from labour, it was the most pain I'd ever been in. James drove me to the hospital, dropped me off and went home with the kids. I made my way to A&E, which was a tent outside the main building as the rest of the hospital was a COVID ward.

I was wearing a face mask, but it felt unbearable. I was hot and felt like I couldn't breathe, making me panicky. The masks also made communicating harder for me. I struggle to hear people through a mask, and I have delayed processing and that requires me to listen, lip read and read people's body language to be able to hear them sometimes.

I told the lady at reception that I thought I'd dislocated my shoulder and was informed that there was a two-hour wait.

When I was eventually seen, I felt so overwhelmed that I burst into tears. I was having a conversation, face-to-face, with someone who wasn't my husband or my kids. Real human interaction that I'd missed so much.

The nurse asked if I was in pain, then said, 'I don't think it's dislocated...'

'Well, it was until my husband popped it back in!'

'Oh, in that case you need to go for an X-ray, but we don't do those here at the moment, so you'll need to go to the other hospital', she told me.

I didn't mind getting a taxi across the city – it meant I could speak to another person! The taxi driver wasn't chatty, so I chewed the ear off the receptionist at the next hospital, where I then had a three-hour wait. Not welcome news.

My phone battery was almost dead. There were no magazines or books in the waiting area. All I had to read were the noticeboards and pamphlets about cancer and stroke. I took a selfie of myself and my poorly arm. Then my phone died.

When I finally had my X-ray, it confirmed a subluxation (a fancy word for partial dislocation). 'You're lucky your husband popped it back in', the doctor told me.

All I could think was that I'd have preferred some strong painkillers beforehand! The doctor put my arm in a sling and sent me home.

HARD TIMES

The next few weeks were brutal. I could barely use my arm, James had to return to work, and the kids still treated me like a climbing frame. Sleep was awful, and every move was agony.

TikTok became my escape – I started making my own videos to pass the time. But mentally, I was drowning. Juggling two kids, a struggling business and a global pandemic was hard enough – now I was down to one functioning arm.

Business was crumbling. Grant money was drying up, sales weren't happening and lockdown dragged on. When restrictions eased in June, some businesses reopened, but social gatherings remained limited. Then came *Eat Out to Help Out* – a major blow. Why would anyone pay for My VIP Card's 25% restaurant discount when the government was handing out 50% for free?

By September, cases spiked again, but there was a glimmer of hope. *The rule of six* meant I could finally see my friends, and with James classified as a key worker, I got a couple of days of childcare. It felt like things might finally be turning.

 Gems of Wisdom

- When you're in a highly stressful situation, you have to do what you can to get through. Lockdown was extreme and highlighted just how important it is to carve out space for yourself.

- If you feel overwhelmed, get help wherever you can. Keep looking for tasks you can delegate.

Chapter 29

Beautiful Way

Beautiful Way *by You Me at Six – from their album* Suckapunch

This song reminds me that any setbacks or struggles I face don't have to define me but can be used to empower me.

In October, I was approached by an investor who felt like a miracle worker. He offered us £250,000 to cover the business plan for My VIP Card and wanted us to start building an app straight away. We knew our audience wanted an app, so we jumped in. The investor chose the developers for us because he had a previous relationship with them.

Normally, I wouldn't have been happy with this, but they seemed nice enough. Nice is not what you need when creating business relationships though, but more on that shortly.

We started intensive work on the app. The investor started to become cagey. It was a lot of money. He suggested that we run another crowdfunding campaign and said he'd put £100,000 in and we could raise the rest from our community.

Nic had already helped me raise £9,000 in our rewards crowdfunder, and after working so closely together for months, we'd become friends. If we were giving people a slice of the pie, we thought a bigger crowd funder would be possible.

There was a lot to organise and lots of dates and deadlines to remember – not my strong point. Nic and Jo helped me a lot. We paid £5,000 to create a video for the crowdfunder, which we could just about manage with what we had in the bank. It was a massive risk and running the crowdfunder was a full-time job.

After four months of planning, our crowdfunder went live. Our investor was nowhere to be seen. I called. I WhatsApp-ed. I emailed. Nothing. He had ghosted us.

He left us up the creek without a paddle. I don't think I have ever been so stressed out in my life. The challenge with crowdfunding is that you need to have half your target pledged before going live. With our investor gone, we were back to zero.

We scrabbled about trying to get ready to launch. We had another investor who wanted to support so we could just about scrape the money we needed to get started. After six weeks of hard slog, our crowdfunder had gone live and we had raised £86,000. It wasn't as simple as that really; it took a lot of planning, and it basically took over my life. There wasn't a waking second that I wasn't promoting it, and I became sick of the sound of my own voice.

From the outside, it looked like we had smashed it, but we had to lower our target significantly to launch. We needed £250,000 to make the app, and we were well short of that figure.

As if that wasn't bad enough, it turned out the developers we had were complete rogues. It was horrific. We had tech that didn't work and a product that could only be sold when we weren't under lockdown restrictions. All the money we raised went on trying to save the app.

I took out loans to pay Jo and Nic. I started to run my business on a credit card, but there wasn't enough money to make it work. The on–off lockdown restrictions weren't helping. One minute, shops could open; the next, they couldn't. Ben and Harriet had at least gone back to school, which was lucky as I was close to a breakdown and poor Jo and Nic were getting the brunt of it.

What to Do If You Think Your Business Is Failing

- Carry out a SWOT (strengths, weaknesses, opportunities, threats) analysis on your business. Be honest about your current situation, is it worth continuing?

- Think about whether your business is giving you joy or stress. If it's the latter, why bother?

- Work out how much money you need to save the business. Can you do it on a budget? If you need external funding, it's probably not worth it.

- Can you add other revenue streams? Is what you're doing now the best way to make money?

- What could you do instead that could make you more money, prevent you from getting into debt and cause you less stress?

I even developed a new app – *Parenthood* – designed specifically to help parents. My intention was to diversify the business so that I could continue making some money. My VIP Card was failing. Not only was it not making me any money, it was actually costing me money, and I needed to do something.

I used the revenue from my parenting forum to get the *Parenthood* app off the ground, but the truth is that it was never my passion.

I couldn't see any way forward, but I kept pushing. I later found out the investor who had ghosted us had invested in one of our competitors. I think his plan all along had been to try and break us. But I wasn't ready to admit defeat.

💎 Gems of Wisdom

- **Research investors properly:** ADHD impulsivity can make us jump in too fast. Due diligence is *not* optional (trust me, I learned the hard way!).

- **Do you even need investment?** Bootstrapping means making money for *you*, not someone else – plus, it's way more fun.

- **Delegate what drains you:** ADHD brains struggle with everything-at-once mode. Play to your strengths and get help where needed.

- **TikTok is ADHD gold:** Fast-paced, dopamine-friendly and perfect for building an engaged audience who actually *want* to buy from you.

Chapter 30

Iris

Iris *by the Goo Goo Dolls – from their album*
Dizzy Up the Girl

This song is about resilience, vulnerability and self-discovery in the face of failure.

It was time to accept the business wasn't working. I had to reverse the franchise. They weren't selling, and it was taking too much of my time. I refunded what I could, which put the business even further into a black hole. The business was now in nearly £80,000 of debt.

I had to make Nic and Jo redundant. I was gutted. This was made even harder by the fact that I'd blurred the boundaries, and we were friends.

I went to my investors and told them that we had no other option but to sell the assets and liquidate the business. I was heartbroken. The business I had worked on for five years was dead. The investors were not happy, which I understood. They were losing their money. But I was losing my livelihood, and my health was at stake. I was in a really bad place mentally and physically.

But it was about to get worse.

PLUMMETING BACK INTO DEBT

The liquidators then gave me terrible news – all the remaining business debt, which amounted to £45,000 was personally guaranteed. That meant I was liable for all of it! This was worse than when I was a student. I was devastated that after all of my hard work to pay off my debt, and stay out of debt, that I'd gone backwards.

I'd thought I was protected as it was a limited company, but it turned out I'd signed for personal guarantees.

For flump's sake* Maddy! I thought to myself. How could I have been so naive? How could I have not read the small print? I was sure I had, but clearly not well enough.

One of my investors had even suggested it to me, and I used his affiliate link to sign up. I was so scared of losing the business that I did what I could to

save it. At the time it felt like the only way.
Hindsight is a fuzzing* wonderful thing. Or maybe
the devil.

As I write this, I am still paying the debt off. I'm a bit
more chilled than last time, and I am in control, but it's
still tough.

I started to spiral. I received death threats from
people who had invested in the crowdfunding because
they had lost money. I was called a fraudster online.
I was bullied online by people who I don't even know
to the point where I had to get the police involved.

I dreaded waking up in the mornings, what was going
to be next?

I did what I could to save it, would it have failed
if it wasn't for the pandemic? Who knows! But
I tried my best.

Don't Beat Yourself Up

Failure is something you can learn from, and it will
help you move forward. It often doesn't feel like it
at the time, but the word 'FAIL' stands for 'First
Attempt in Learning'.

But I was the bad guy. I lost friends, and I had to do a
handover with the business that bought the assets,
which meant travelling to the Cotswolds one day a
week. I really resented the travel, I resented the business. I just didn't want anything more to do with it.

I had handed over what I could, although there wasn't much to hand over, just my contacts and business plans. It was giving me trauma. The words 'My VIP Card' gave me the shivers. Luckily the people who took over wanted to get rid of the name too.

How to Get Out of Victim Mode

Motivational speaker and coach Taz Thornton shared the following advice to help you break out of victim mode and take control.

- **Flip negatives:** Reframe your mindset by asking: *Why did this happen to me? What's now possible? What did I learn?*

- **Practice gratitude:** List five things you're grateful for every morning (or 10 if you struggle!).

- **Set your mood at night:** Before bed, affirm that your sleep will reset your mind, body and spirit for a great day ahead.

- **Set daily intentions:** Write down a positive focus for the day where you'll see it.

- **Change your state:** Move! Dance, run, lift weights or blast music and sing – physical shifts boost your mindset.

AT A CROSSROADS

What the fresh merry hell* was I going to do now? I tried to look for jobs, but I just wasn't interested in

any of them, and working for someone else while
doing the handover wasn't helping.

The idea of going to work for someone else filled me
with dread. I had been self-employed for over
six years, successfully at times, although there were
other times when I had to decide whether to eat or
pay a bill (I always chose eating, obviously!).

On the one hand, I thought having a guaranteed salary
would be good, but on the other hand I just couldn't
face the idea of not fitting in again, of having to conform and dye my hair a regular colour. I'm just not a
regular sort of person.

I love being able to manage my own day, work when
I want and have my afternoon nap, which is essential.
I genuinely think I am unemployable! (If you are
reading this and I have fluffed up yet another business
I take this back.)

I remember feeling really stupid for being so upset
about losing a business. But when I unpacked it,
I realised that feeling upset was justified. I had dedicated five years of my life to it, and I loved it. I had
hyperfocused on it every day for as long as I could
remember. It was an important part of my journey, and
one that my kids had been part of too. I needed to let
myself feel the emotions to process them.

I was still in hell, and it was all so raw. I felt like a total
failure, I felt like the one thing I had going for me was

this business, and I couldn't even get that right. I was really struggling, and as if the business folding wasn't bad enough, as a family, we received some devastating news.

💎 Gems of Wisdom

- **Reframe failure:** ADHD brains thrive on new perspectives. If something flops, pivot and find another way. Rock bottom just means there's only one way to go – *up!*

- **Clients leaving?** It's not about you. They're making space for the right people who *actually* value what you do.

- **One setback ≠ the end:** ADHD rejection sensitivity hits hard, but remember: resilience is your superpower.

- **Nothing is final:** Business (like ADHD) is all about adapting. Nothing is un-fixable.

Chapter 31

Dancing Queen

Dancing Queen *by ABBA – from their album* Arrival

This song is dedicated to my mother-in-law, as it was her favourite. But it also represents the time when I started to get to know who I really was and felt free to dance to my own tune.

At the beginning of November, I found out that my mother-in-law Jenny was really poorly. She had end-stage liver disease. They had given her three years to live, and we were all devastated. But by the end of November, she was so sick that she couldn't keep anything down, and James's brother had to call an ambulance.

James rushed down to Devon to be with her. He was there for two weeks. I had to get my mum to help with the kids because I was working one day a week in the Cotswolds to do the handover for the business.

One week after Jenny was admitted to hospital, they said she could go home. But when it came to discharging her, they found something else wrong. She started to deteriorate really quickly.

It was a Saturday when James called me. 'You need to come now, I think this is the end', he said. I called my mum to ask her to have the kids for me. On Monday morning, I drove for five hours to get to Jenny's village, Bratton Clovelly.

James was at the hospital when I arrived, so I had to hunt for the spare key in the spider-infested shed. That was traumatic on its own. Once I'd dropped my things off, I drove to Exeter Hospital, where James met me at the entrance.

It felt like the longest walk ever along the corridor to his mum's ward. I was not prepared for what awaited me. Jenny looked so poorly. Jaundice had set in, her skin, eyes and nails were all a funny mustard colour. She was dipping in and out of consciousness. I went for a coffee and a bit of cake with Claire, James' cousin, and we chatted a bit. I gave Jenny a little hand squeeze and we drove back to Bratton for the night.

It was December. Jenny's hope was to make it to Christmas, but it wasn't looking likely. In the morning,

James and I drove back to the hospital in separate cars as I'd need to leave to pick the kids up that evening.

The doctor met us when we arrived and said she wasn't doing well, and that her organs were starting to fail. James went to get a cup of tea, and I had some time alone with Jenny. She was still dipping in and out of consciousness, but she knew I was there. She opened her eyes, and I felt so scared for her that I asked if she was in any pain. She mumbled, 'no'.

It was hard to understand her, which was really upsetting. 'Make sure James is ok', she said.

'I will look after him forever, I promise', I replied, and she squeezed my hand.

I told her that I loved her, and she was the best mother-in-law I could have asked for.

Knowing that was the last time I would ever see Jenny hit me really hard. It was horrendous knowing that she was going to die and that I wouldn't ever be able to have random chats with her on the phone where she told me which dogs or tractors were passing her window. I had never had to actually say goodbye to anyone before. Everyone I knew who'd died had done so unexpectedly. Saying goodbye to someone is so hard.

I left the hospital crying my eyes out, and I cried all the way home. I was exhausted mentally. When I arrived at my mum's to pick up the kids, they had just sat down to eat. Mum had enough food for me too.

'How is nannie mummy?' Ben asked.

'She isn't good, bud', I replied.

'Is she going to die, mummy?'

'Sadly yes, she is, darling', I replied.

This prompted a very difficult but amusing conversation about death, and Ben's theories about where people go when they die – to a big pub in the sky apparently! Sort of concerning coming from a six year old!

I took them home, tucked them into bed and kissed them goodnight. Harriet demanded 'strokies', which is her standard sensory thing for helping her to sleep. I don't blame her, it's mine too.

They had been asleep for about half an hour, when the phone rang. It was James, 'She's gone', he said.

I burst into tears. I was terrified of telling the kids that nannie had died. I think that was the hardest thing I had to do, even though I knew they would cope, possibly better than me.

As I mentioned in Chapter 15, when you have ADHD you feel grief **hard**. Emotional regulation is really tough when you have ADHD, so grief can lead to bad habits creeping in – like drinking or spending too much. It can also disrupt your routine, and the physical stress can really impact your body. This loss was so sudden that we barely had time to process it. But we had to accept that she was gone. We had lost James's dad only a few years earlier and that was even more sudden.

Now I had to try and push aside my feelings to support James, he had lost two parents in the space of three years, which was just heartbreaking. And he was so close to both of them.

How to Deal with Grief

These tips come from Karen Whybrow, a grief coach: karenwhybrow.com

- **Grieve at your pace:** It's messy and nonlinear; let yourself feel it.

- **Be kind to yourself:** Prioritise self-care and accept that it's OK to not be OK.

- **Accept support:** Lean on loved ones and seek help when needed.

- **Stay busy if helpful:** Distraction can help, but take breaks when needed.

- **Honour their memory:** Talk about them, share stories and keep them close.

- **Do what feels right:** Your grief journey is yours – there are no rules.

James had to stay in Devon to sort out arrangements for Jenny's funeral. It was really tough dealing with the grief of her passing, whilst looking after the kids, and trying to go to work. At this point, I was still doing a handover to the people who bought the assets of My VIP Card. But in some ways James being away was actually helpful so I could process my own grief.

Losing Jenny really gave me a reality check. I was grieving for a business, something that was totally material, and her passing made me see there were much more important things than a business. Yes, I was sad. But I needed to get over it. My grief was needed elsewhere now.

Grief is a really funny thing, you can't control it, especially with ADHD. I was also in victim mode. I kept asking why was all this happening to me? Why was I a serial blunderer*? I was in a mess; mentally everything was crumbling around me. I had no idea how I was going to pay all the debt back and I didn't know where to turn. I felt so alone.

 Gems of Wisdom

- Grief is really hard to deal with when you have ADHD. Be kind to yourself and be aware that the strong emotions you're feeling could mean you fall back into bad habits.
- Talk about how you're feeling to someone you trust. Don't keep it all bottled up.
- And allow yourself to feel and cry; bottled up tears weigh down the heart.

Chapter 32

Find Me

> **Find Me *by Kings of Leon – from their album* Walls**
>
> This has one of the best intros of any song I've ever heard. One of my hyperfocuses is to listen to the intro. It gives me all the dopamine.

Not long after Jenny passed away, the person who had bought My VIP Card's assets asked me to stay on at the company and run it as its CEO. What the fuzz*?! It was a hard no. I told him where he could stick his job and walked out. There may have been a few FBombs!

With no money coming in and, even worse, a mountain of debt, I knew that I needed to do something. I sat down with my CV and managed to bundle my six years of self-employment into something that actually made me sound like I was really blooming employable*, instead of the absolute failure I felt like.

At least that was one useful skill I'd developed from my years in recruitment. I sent my CV to every job that I could do that wasn't paying peanuts. And I waited.

But I'm not good at waiting. What could I do? I couldn't just sit there earning no money at all. I thought maybe I could sign on but that was a major hasslefest*, because the forms are way too compli-cated! I figured I'd probably get a job before they paid me, so I decided against it.

The one highlight at this point was that I was receiving recognition as an individual for the money tips I'd started sharing on *TikTok*. I had time on my hands, so I was sharing personal money-saving tips on *TikTok* every day and people started to pay attention to what I was saying. I was featured in the national press. I was even contacted to be on a documentary for 5* called *Bargain Brits on Benefits*. I'd never thought of *TikTok*, a platform where I made silly videos during the pan-demic, as a place to do business.

When I recorded the documentary, I had 3,000 follow-ers, and I wasn't really taking it seriously. Of course, that all changed, and as I write this, I have over 70,000 followers!

Getting Started on *Tiktok*

- **TikTok is for everyone:** If you can communicate, you can make money (even without speaking!).

- **Pick a niche you love:** Something you'll still enjoy in five years.

- **Use the Stable Table Method:** Stick to four content pillars that support your personal brand.

- **Learn from others:** Collaborate with your niche instead of fearing competition.

- **Mix up content:** Storytelling, education and entertainment work better than constant selling.

- **Join my membership:** Get training and a kick up the bum to get started! Its only £10 a month!

GETTING AWAY

My mum was worried about me, and she told me she was going to take me and the kids to Lapland to visit Father Christmas, or Santa, whatever you want to call him. Expensive! But she paid for the lot. In fact, I didn't even take my purse with me. I had literally not a penny to my name.

Lapland was a welcome break from my grief, which I was still processing for both Jenny and the business. We flew out on 16 December.

It was all about the kids, a trip for them to see the big man himself. I was desperate to see the northern lights, but I had been told the chances were about as good as seeing rocking horse poo! Apparently even if you were in the right place, often they couldn't be seen with the naked eye.

We had a full-on day on the Santa tour. We went in an igloo, we watched a little show, we went on a reindeer ride (which Harri hated) and we went sledding, which all of us broadly loved. But Harri had been a night-mare all day – it was minus 25 °C and her gloves kept falling off because she had teeny hands.

We even went on a husky ride, which I found awful. The smell was terrible, and my mum's sleigh driving was so bad that I nearly fell off at one point. It was a highly sensory day, and I realised both myself and the kids are very sensory aware. We don't like being too hot or too cold, and we don't like loud noises and overwhelming smells. We were knackered when we got back.

At dinner that evening, we met a lovely couple who I decided to share a bottle of wine with. I had down-loaded the *Aurora* app on my iPhone, which sent alerts for Aurora Borealis. Whilst we were eating din-ner, there was an alert that in an hour we may see them.

My mum knew how excited I was about the potential to see them, so she took the kids to bed so I could go to the viewing gallery. I carried on drinking. I sat in the viewing gallery with the lovely couple from

dinner, drinking wine and staring up at the stars.
Even if we didn't see them, I was still having a really
good laugh.

We waited for about an hour. People started to leave
the viewing gallery, but I was there for the long haul.

All of a sudden, I could see something in the sky.
There were literally no clouds, you could see all the
stars. Then there was this shape. It looked a bit like
smoke. A haze that almost looked like it was shooting
up from the trees. We stared at it, and it started to get
bigger and longer, and then it started to change colour.
I could actually see it with my naked eyes! It was a lot
better and clearer with my phone. But I was seeing the
northern lights before my eyes. It was a dream come
true, something I never thought I would ever see.

I honestly can't explain the happiness that was going
through my body. I was on cloud nine, every ounce of
me felt happy and free. I wasn't sure if the northern
lights were something you could manifest on, but
I was going to fuzzing* try. I stared at them whilst
repeating in my mind 'This Too Shall Pass' I envisaged
myself surrounded by light and in a better place and it
gave me comfort.

I want all of this pain to go away, and I want to be
successful, that was all I asked for. I am a big believer
in asking the universe for things. In fact, I feel like
I have manifested a lot of things. The most brilliant
streak of green light filled the sky.

The next day I got just as much of a high showing the other hotel guests my pictures of what I had seen. I was in the right place, at the right time. Everyone was asking me to send them my pictures, which I thought was a bit weird, but I obliged.

It turned out that they hadn't been seen in our hotel for two weeks, and it was actually not a particularly good time to see them. I felt like it was meant to be.

In the moment I saw those lights, I felt something happen to me. I had an overwhelming gratitude; I felt so thankful for being alive. In that moment, I decided I was absolutely sick of my current circumstances, and I needed to change my life.

I realised after getting back from Lapland that I had transferred my grief from one thing to another. Jenny dying so suddenly had been a wake-up call for me. I couldn't carry on the way I was; life was too short to be wallowing. I needed to take action.

Christmas was sucky; it was sad. Jenny had spent the last eight Christmases with us, or we had gone to hers. It just felt empty. I don't think either me or James had really started to process our grief.

But after I'd got back from the Lapland trip, I started to think more about my well-being and how I could start to change my life around. I knew it had to start with self-care.

MIND, BODY AND SOUL TIPS FOR SELF-CARE

Jennifer Mckenzie, Somatic Trauma Therapist at www.lunarspiritwellbeing.com, shared these tips to help you develop a better self-care routine.

- **Get to know yourself:** ADHD traits vary, so self-discovery is key. A new diagnosis can be a shake-up, so start observing your thoughts and behaviours.

- **Make it fun:** Journal or scrapbook to explore what makes you feel good and what doesn't. This helps with unmasking and self-advocacy.

- **Reframe intrusive thoughts:** They're common, but they're not you. Replace *'No one likes me'* with *'My brain is lying – plus, I've got a to-do list, so no cliff jumping today'*. Say it out loud!

- **Breathe!** ADHD brains often live in fight-or-flight mode. Try deep belly breathing – inhale for 5, exhale for 8 – to calm your nervous system.

- **Move daily:** Dance, walk, cycle – whatever works! Moving helps regulate emotions. I call it *'dancing with my emotions'* – it shifts stress, anger or zoomy energy.

- **Invest in therapy:** It helps with past trauma, self-esteem and setting boundaries. Late diagnosis often means years of unprocessed struggles – release them to thrive.

- **Find your people:** Community makes all the difference. Your ADHD brain is incredible – you are incredible! Maddy's membership is perfect for this!

Gems of Wisdom

- Sometimes we need a change of scene to gain perspective on a situation – or someone who can help lift us out of a pit of self-despair.

- Sometimes you need to put yourself first, it's okay to be selfish.

Chapter 33

What You Know

What You Know *by Two Door Cinema Club –*
from their album Tourist History

This is one of the most positive songs I've ever
come across. While I was writing this book,
I kept hearing it everywhere. It's got a great
message of growth and resilience in the face of
disappointment.

I was so happy when the kids went back to school and
nursery after the pandemic. Ben had a new teacher,
who seemed a lot more invested than the teachers
he'd had previously. When I collected him from school,
she'd tell me about the things he was doing, which
just didn't seem right.

Initially, I wasn't sure if it was just because he'd become used to being at home during the pandemic, but the more she spoke to me about him and his behaviour, the more I thought it was worth investigating.

One day, she took me aside and said, 'He does handstands when he is supposed to be doing maths. He doodles all the time. He is constantly swinging on his chair. He gets up and walks around all the time. He is very emotional. He distracts the class – he isn't naughty as such Mrs Alexander-Grout, but I do think you should consider that Ben may have ADHD'.

ADHD? But ADHD is for naughty little boys… I decided I needed to learn everything, so I took to Google straight away. I started looking at what ADHD looked like in boys. I had so many questions. How did he get it? Was I giving him too much sugar? Was he having too much screen time? (Both of these are total myths by the way, although both can exacerbate ADHD symptoms.)

Google wasn't particularly helpful, so I went to *TikTok*. It turned out to be the best thing I ever decided to do!

It was March 2022, and I totally fell down the *TikTok* rabbit hole. I found ADHD Tok and I never came out. I started to watch videos from content creators all about ADHD, and they were so relatable!

I wasn't convinced Ben had it, but very quickly I was nodding along to all of the videos going 'oh, oh, that's me!' I really identified with everything all of the content creators were saying. In my mind, I just knew it: I have ADHD.

LIGHTBULB MOMENTS

I spent about eight weeks writing down all of the things I related to, which was basically anything I could find on *TikTok*. It was like a lightbulb had gone off in my brain and I suddenly felt accepted, validated and the least like a chaos conductor* I had ever felt in my life.

My world felt aligned. I wasn't useless. I wasn't a broken horse. I was a beautiful rainbow zebra, and I had ADHD.

The next thing I did was work out how I could get a diagnosis. I filled in some online questionnaires to see what my likelihood of having ADHD was, and they came back 100% every time.

My friend Liz had ADHD, so I spoke to her. She replied, 'MATE!! How on earth have you never thought about it before?!' She was also convinced I had ADHD. Now I could have seen this as insulting, I often come across people I meet now who I suspect have ADHD and, whilst I don't diagnose them, I sometimes mention it. This is not me trying to be rude. It has changed my life so much. I really welcomed her feedback.

When you understand your brain it's honestly a game changer.

Then I had a call with a lady who went through my childhood markers with me. These are the signs I had ADHD that were present during my childhood. We went through all of my school reports. Here's a sample for you...

'Maddy would do better if she stopped daydreaming' – **Sorry I'm not listening, I'm thinking about what I'm having for my tea**.

'Maddy is inept at physical education' – **Physical what?**

'Maddy gets distracted easily' – **Erm, is that a unicorn?**

'Maddy struggles to maintain friendships' – **Harsh, but fair!**

'Maddy is extremely focused on subjects that she likes but will not apply herself to subjects like maths and science' – **Give me art any day!**

'Maddy talks a lot, she distracts other classmates and herself. She always forgets her homework, or it looks rushed and substandard' – **Erm, the dog ate it!**

So, what can we pick out here? Easily distracted, hyperfocus, lack of coordination and forgetfulness, just to name a few.

The more I looked into ADHD, the more convinced I was that I had it. Not only that, but it was starting to help me to make sense of why I was a walking disaster zone*.

My debt problems, my ridiculous overattachment to certain people, my previous relationships, my people pleasing, my inability to hold down a job, my oversharing, my constant interruptions of other people talking, my quest for dopamine in so many different ways!

I wasn't terrible at everything! I just had a different operating system! I was a tape! A tape that was unravelling while being forced into a CD player.

I was a freaking tape! Every time I played, I unravelled. I needed to be rewound to work again. This concept has resonated with me so much that I've had a tattoo of this image done while I've been writing this book.

As you'll have noticed, music in particular has been an anchor for me my whole life. It's a mood changer. If you're feeling low, putting on your favourite song and having a dance around or listening to a song that reminds you of a different time is so powerful.

I also love how music brings us together. The reason I've always loved going to a gig or festival is that it creates a sense of belonging to a group of people who all like the same thing. It creates a sense of community, and community has always been one of my values.

Music was also my hyperfocus, especially when I was younger. I'd record the charts every Sunday, and heaven forbid anyone interrupted me. Music helped me feel more normal, and it was a good conversation starter at school when I had no idea what to talk to people about. I learnt about every band and artist I could, and I've carried that knowledge with me ever since. My husband and I even watch *Top of the Pops* reruns every Friday as our date night, just so we can talk about bands we like.

MAKING IT OFFICIAL

I wanted an official diagnosis desperately enough that I paid to go private. Only I was a bloody cheapskate and only paid £470 for it – which doesn't sound cheap, but compared to most ADHD diagnosis options, it is.

I had an hour-long interview with someone, and they said, 'Yes, you have ADHD.'

OK, it was as easy as that! Now that I knew I had ADHD, I could start owning it and telling people I have it. I was actually quite excited about having the label, because it brought validation and helped me make sense of my life.

Now I could tell people that I wasn't just weird or rude! It was like the most colourful lightbulb had gone 'click' in my head.

TIPS FOR DIAGNOSIS

There are various support services available to help diagnose ADHD for your child, or for yourself as an adult.

- **Speak to your doctor:** They'll be able to refer you for an ADHD diagnosis; ask to be referred through a 'right to choose pathway'.

- **Contact CAMHS:** This is the Child and Adolescent Mental Health Services in the UK. You can go directly to CAMHS for a referral, or your child's school can refer them to CAMHS for a diagnosis.

- **Get a private diagnosis:** Organisations like ADHD 360 provide ADHD diagnosis and support. You can get a diagnosis through certain private organisations using Right to Choose. If you're in the UK, check whether you're eligible for the NHS Right to Choose as this means you won't pay for the assessment. If you're looking for an assessment for your child, make sure any provider you approach offers children's assessments as well as adult ones.

Whatever route to diagnosis you go down, do your research. I know that can feel like a painful process, but trust me, it's worth it!

Also, this process is definitely not neurodivergent-friendly! So, if you've got ADHD (or suspect you do), it can feel overwhelming to have to fill in a load of forms about your child having ADHD. My top tip is to find someone who can sit with you and talk through the answers.

I did this process with my husband when we did our son's CAMHS referral, and that really helped.

I know that there can be some stigma around receiving an ADHD diagnosis, and the media definitely hasn't helped with that. But I want you to know that there's no shame in having ADHD. It's not your fault. It's not your parents' fault. There's nothing wrong with you. It's just that the world has given us a cassette tape, but we've got a CD player in our heads. So, we've got to learn how we can convert what we're presented with to work with our operating system.

If you suspect you've got ADHD, the likelihood is that you probably do. If you've done enough research on the symptoms and how it presents in others to see signs of it in yourself, then I believe that's worth looking into no matter how old you are. For me, getting a diagnosis was a chance to learn how to better manage in this world and it validated my feelings of being different.

But getting a diagnosis as an adult is a personal choice, so do what you feel will best support *you*.

Tips If You Think Your Child Has ADHD

The following is some excellent advice from Lauren O'Carroll, an ADHD parenting specialist.

- **Track symptoms:** Note behaviours at home and school to support diagnosis.

- **Know the process:** Research diagnosis steps in your country; in the UK, check **Right to Choose**.

- **Use ADHD-friendly parenting:** Focus on evidence-based strategies and being their safe space.

- **Look after yourself:** Self-care matters; you can't support them if you're running on empty.

FOCUSING ON MY FAMILY

Of course, it was Ben's teacher's observations about his behaviour that set this whole chain of events in motion. After I realised that I had ADHD by looking at Ben's and Harriet's little quirks, it became more obvious that they were so similar to me.

Lauren O'Carroll has also shared some signs of ADHD at different points in a child's life.

I lived in constant worry of being a terrible parent because I was so overwhelmed all the time. Even once we were on the other side of the pandemic, dealing with two kids I still felt like I could barely look after

Early Signs of ADHD in Children

Babies: Constant crying, fussiness, frustration, feeding issues, sleep struggles and needing constant contact (or avoiding it).

Toddlers and Preschoolers: Intense, long tantrums, emotional extremes, impatience, difficulty transitioning, quick frustration, sensory sensitivities, rejection sensitivity, overstimulation and strong reactions to boundaries.

myself and small people needed even more. I gave them as much love as I could. I thought about it a lot and realised I knew about my neurodivergent stuff, so I also knew about theirs.

My parents did what I would consider to be an amazing job raising me and my sister because they gave us all the love in the world. And when you have love, nothing else really matters.

They didn't know about ADHD when we were growing up, especially not in girls. I also did a very good job of masking my struggles because I was scared of disappointing my mum. I know she would have done more to support he if I had been honest with her about my mental health worries. I just didn't know how to talk openly.

I wish I had told my mum more of what was going on in my head, because I think it would have helped me. So, I'm encouraging my kids to talk about being neurodivergent, and I am trying to educate them with what I know.

Now that we know more about our brains and mental health, it's become easier to talk about. I want them to know they shouldn't ever feel scared to talk about their neurodivergent condition, or how they're feeling.

Every time I start to worry that I'm a rubbish parent, I remember that someone once said to me that if you think you're a rubbish parent, it means you care enough to not to be one.

With my diagnosis, I suddenly knew more about myself, which meant I had a lot of knowledge I could share not only with my kids, but with everyone else too.

💎 Gems of Wisdom

- If you think you have any neurodivergent condition, start learning about it. Understanding why you are struggling can help.

- Keep a diary of what you struggle with, in personal and business life, and gather evidence like your old school reports to see if you can find any signs.

- Speak to people who have known you for a while, especially those who have known you since childhood.

- Getting an ADHD diagnosis is a personal choice, but I've found it incredibly helpful to connect with others in the neurodivergent community.

Chapter 34

Keep Your Head Up

> **Keep Your Head Up** *by Ben Howard – from his album* **Every Kingdom**
>
> This is a motivational song for anyone who feels like they don't belong. The first time I heard this song, I cried the whole way through.

Getting my ADHD diagnosis had helped me understand myself a lot better, but it didn't change the hard, cold facts of my situation. My business had failed. I was in £45,000 of debt, and I didn't have a job. What was I going to do?

Then, one midnight, I woke up with a brainwave: I could make money out of something I love doing. My brain started ticking over; there was no chance I was going back to sleep now. The main question in my mind was, but what? What did I love doing? And how could I make money from whatever that thing was?

I started a mind map. I put my name on a piece of paper, and I wrote down all of the things I was good at, was interested in, and that made me tick, as well as listing all the things I didn't like doing.

Then it dawned on me. Maybe ADHD had some positives. Maybe I could use my skills and my strengths to be outrageously awesome at something!

During the pandemic, I had paid to do a course called *One to Many* with Lisa Johnson. I had hoped it would be a magic pill to save My VIP Card, but it didn't work for several reasons – I went into the course in desperation mode, I wasn't thinking outside of the box or trusting the process, and if I was completely honest, I knew at that point My VIP Card was beyond saving.

However, I had lifetime access to the course, so I watched it all again.

I was in the zone! I wrote down all of the things that gave me joy. I wanted to help as many people as I could to improve their money situation, but I also wanted to help business owners. Then it dawned on me – I had been coaching people for many years. My *TikTok* channel was flying – I had 25,000 followers. I was sharing money tips, and talking about my experiences with debt and spending. But what I hadn't talked about so far was ADHD.

FINDING MY CALLING

Out of the blue, someone contacted me to ask if I did money coaching. I hadn't really done money coaching before, but I agreed to speak to his daughter as she wanted to move out and get her money in line.

As soon as I spoke to her, I knew I had found my calling. I had a skill I could use to help people. I decided that I would start a coaching business to help people who have ADHD with their money and their businesses. Then I had an idea to create a community for people who have ADHD where they can learn and support each other – that's when *Mad About Money* was born, although I hadn't settled on the name just yet.

What You Need to Know Before You Start a Coaching Business (That Nobody Tells You)

Sara Parsons, who is a mentor for coaches (www.saraparsons.com), has some fantastic advice if, like me, you think coaching could be your calling.

- **You are your best marketing tool:** People buy from people, not perfect websites. Show up authentically.

- **Niche down:** Trying to help everyone waters down your impact. Focus on a specific audience to attract the right clients.

(continued)

- **Mindset is key:** Resilience and adaptability matter just as much as strategy.

- **Social proof builds trust:** offering a few free sessions can help you gather testimonials.

- **Automate early:** Streamline lead generation, audience growth and income to avoid overwhelm.

OVERCOMING THE DOUBTS AND HATERS

When I launched the *Mad About Money* app, I got a lot of stick from people who accused me of 'starting a phoenix business' and just changing the name of My VIP Card. But that couldn't have been further from the truth. *Mad About Money* was completely different, and built using my *TikTok* audience, not any existing connections from My VIP Card.

I knew that it was a different concept, but it was still hard to ignore some of the hate coming in my direction. I knew I wanted to help people with ADHD to have their own businesses and thrive. But I had imposter syndrome. I kept asking myself, who wants to learn business from someone with a failed one? As it turns out, quite a lot of people!

I also knew that I wanted a dedicated app that could be a place that helped people wherever they were in their money journey. I wanted to build a

community, where people supported each other.
I started planning.

As I mentioned earlier, when My VIP Card started to
fail, I developed the *Parenthood* app, which was a
good idea for supporting parents, but it gave me no
joy and running it was hard. My friend Kathy, who runs
an amazing employee benefits platform called *Healthy
Minds Club*, bought Parenthood from me, which gave
me what I needed to invest in building the *Mad About
Money* app.

With my *TikTok* following over 35,000, it was fairly easy
to get people invested in what I was doing. But these
were people with money problems, and I knew
I couldn't charge them to access the app. I started
building anyway and trusted that making money would
come later. I used Ugenie, which is run by my friend
Susan, to build my community space.

I designed about 300 different logos. I bought about
20 domains. I couldn't decide what to call my community and app.

I wanted somewhere people would feel safe to talk
about money and life; somewhere they could go to ask
questions and get tips. I wanted it to be fun and
friendly. After coming up with dozens of ideas, 'Mad
About Money' was the winner. It's a play on my name,
but also a play on the word 'mad'. I wanted the slogan
to be 'You don't have to be mad to be here, but it
helps'. I was a bit worried people wouldn't see the

funny side of it, but I rolled with it. It's also where the name of this book came from.

But money can make us mad in so many ways. We are madly in love with it, we are cross with it, it makes us feel crazy at times. It just felt right.

I launched *Mad About Money* on 4 May 2023, and it started to fly. My biggest problem was that I had spent a lot of money and time on it, with no real way of making any money back. And I should have charged people from day one. My biggest mistake. It's so much harder to get people to pay for something if they are used to getting it for free.

ADHD AND ENTREPRENEURSHIP

My biggest issue with ADHD and running a business is that I'm great at helping other people, but often I get carried away with a plan and think about the finer details later, which is not really the way to create a business strategy.

I talked earlier about my first entrepreneurial venture – charging other students to change their dates of birth on their student IDs and provisional driving licences – and I acknowledged then that, even though I knew it was illegal, I didn't think through the consequences of my actions.

One of the traits of my ADHD – and it's the same for many ADHDers – is my impulsivity. As you've seen so far, this has got me into a lot of trouble at times. But being impulsive as an entrepreneur presents both challenges and opportunities.

To this day, I know that I still don't weigh up all the options properly. I have a thirst for learning, so I'm constantly signing up for courses and workshops that I don't always have time to complete. But at least that impulsivity is allowing me to learn new things.

With my last business – My VIP Card – I took out a lot of debt without reading the small print or thinking about the consequences. That obviously had a significant negative knock-on impact on the rest of my life. What I've got much better at since then is building my awareness. So, I know that I can be impulsive and although I don't always get it right, I'm much better at taking a step back and understanding when I'm behaving in this way.

A case in point was an event I was due to attend when I was writing this book. I'd said yes to it without considering that it was a three-hour round trip for me to get there, I had just got home from two back-to-back festivals and was shattered, and I had no childcare for the evening. In the end, I contacted the organisers, apologised and explained I couldn't attend because I had made an impulsive decision.

My ability to hyperfocus means that, when I sit down to get work done, I get things done really quickly. I'm very creative and spontaneous, which means I can do things off the cuff and do them well. I'm constantly coming up with new ideas, but I'm very conscious that as an ADHD entrepreneur I have a million ideas, so I need to be selective about which ones I focus on. It doesn't mean I don't have days where my head is mush and I can't function, but for the majority I use my ADHD to harness good in my business because I play to my strengths.

Advice for an Impulsive Entrepreneur

Focus fuels growth! ADHD makes it tough, but honing in on one idea at a time works wonders. Minimise distractions and ensure everything aligns with your personal brand.

One of the benefits to my coaching clients is that I have too many ideas for business to enact myself, so I naturally share them with those around me. Because I understand the challenges and opportunities ADHD brings to entrepreneurs, I'm an awesome coach for people who have neurodivergent conditions, because I can help them better understand how their own brains work and in doing so help them continue to take meaningful steps forward in their business every day.

REMEMBER, YOUR BRAIN IS DIFFERENT

One of my biggest tips for neurodivergent entrepreneurs is to stop following advice from neurotypical gurus, they don't learn in the same way we do, and also it makes us feel like we can't do things, then we feel like we are failing.

It can be really easy to wonder, 'Why isn't this working for me?' when the truth is that you and the 'guru' you're trying to emulate are completely different people. Many of us are solopreneurs, who either don't have or can't afford teams yet. The earlier you can understand how your brain works, the sooner you'll be able to build a strong foundation on which you can build a successful business.

These are also all good reasons why you should work with an ADHD business coach. Not only do we understand your brain, which means we can help create strategies that work for you and your business, but we can help you work out what your strengths are and how to work with them.

ADHD business coaches will also be able to help you find opportunities to work with other neurodivergent business owners, and they will know about schemes like *Access to Work* in the UK that can help pay for the cost of having a coach. The majority of my clients are funded through *Access to Work*.

HOW TO START A BUSINESS WHEN YOU HAVE ADHD

It's really common for people who have ADHD to not want to work for other people, because we often have years of trauma, but how do we actually do that?

- Start by finding your niche. I find it helps to think about these things:

What does the world need?

What can I be paid for?

What do I love doing?

What am I good at?

Find your business sweet spot in the middle of all these things

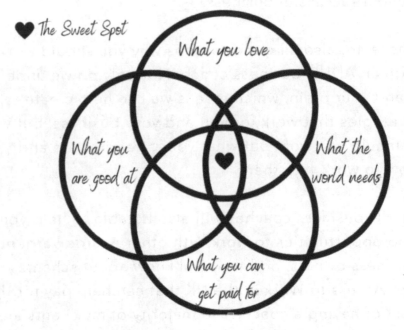

- What is the essence of your brand?

What do you stand for?

What are your values?

What is your mission?

What is your vision?

- Who do you want to work with? And how do you reach them? This can't just be 'women' or 'people with ADHD' – you need to get down and dirty and create an ideal client avatar. Give them a name, think about:

Where they shop.

What they eat.

Where they hang out.

What their favourite social platforms are.

How old they are.

What TV shows they watch.

It's so much easier to sell to someone when you have a specific person in mind.

- What do you sell? Think about how to package up your services so that they appeal to your ideal clients. The trick is to keep it simple! I follow this process:

  - **Something free:** You need something free to give away to your audience that will get them into your world in exchange for their email address.

  - **Something low cost:** This could be an e-book, a guide, a planner or a short workshop or similar.

  - **Something one-to-one:** Only if you want to work one-to-one that is.

  - **Something high ticket:** This might be a mastermind, an event or a longer course.

- Think about why people should work with you.

  What do you bring to the table?

  What is the problem you are solving for your client?

What is the solution you can give them?

It's OK for you to want to have multiple streams of income but try and make sure they all relate back to you.

- Think personal brand. I am a multi-potentialite, which means I do lots of stuff for lots of people. It just so happens they are all neurodivergent, which all ties to my personal brand. Creating a personal brand helps you when you are neurodivergent and you want to do all of the things, because we often get bored and want to change what we are doing. If you make it all about you, it's easier to pivot if you want to without having to start from scratch.

- How do you price it all? This is the bit more people struggle with.
  - **First, check out your competition:** See what they are selling, and at what price.

  - **Consider your experience compared to them:** You are unlikely to sell a £10,000 coaching package if you have never coached before, for instance.

  - **Think about your time:** How much were you getting paid in your corporate job? Work out how many clients you need to see one-to-one, or how many packages you need to sell to make that money or more.

  - **Dream big! You've got this:** Think about the value you bring to that person.

  - **Think about your audience:** What do you think they can afford?

- **Test the water:** Find your ideal clients and float your pricing by them. Do your market research.

- **Do you:** A person who walks alone gets further ahead, so stop following the crowd or doing what you 'think' you should do to run a business.

- Stop following the neurotypical gurus. They don't understand how your brain works and building a business when you have ADHD is so different!

LOOKING UP

With *Mad About Money* taking off, it felt like things were finally starting to go right for me. I still had a failed business, a fruit bowl* of ailments and debts piled higher than I could manage, but I finally felt like I was moving forwards.

One of the things that really helped me to move on was manifesting – yeah, I know more hippy-dippy stuff. I didn't really resonate with the ones I found online though, so I created my own – ones that supported my ADHD brain and helped me to feel more positively about my life, my money and my situation.

My ADHD Money Manifestations/Affirmations

- Money flows to me because my ADHD has all the ideas.

- I am worthy of earning more money, I just take a more unique approach.

(continued)

- I am an ADHD money magnet.

- My income is growing as I build my knowledge of ADHD.

- I know my stuff and can help others with ADHD to fly.

- My ADHD isn't a superpower, but my hyperfocus helps me to grow.

- My ADHD comes with great strengths, and I use them to help people.

- My money and business improve every day because of my creativity and hyperfocus.

- My neurodivergent conditions only stand in the way if I let them.

- My brain is unique to me and can help me achieve great things.

- I achieve my goals one step at a time.

- My ADHD makes me resilient AF.

- I embrace challenges, learn from failure and continue to grow.

Mad About Money is a fabulous community – I often refer to it as my really expensive lead funnel. It's the best freebie ever! The reason it works is that it brings people into my world in a central place. It's also been amazing for generating interest in the press and helping me find new partnerships. Along with my *TikTok*, this community also brings me many new clients.

It feels like a win-win. I get to help everyone, and those who want a bit more of my time and personalised advice, give something back to me by using my coaching services.

💎 Gems of Wisdom

- If you don't know where to start with a new business, use a mind map. Think about who you are, what you love and what will bring you joy, then go from there. You can also use ChatGPT to help you to throw ideas around.

- Building a coaching business has been great for me, but there's more to it than just showing up on sessions. Whatever kind of business you want to start, do thorough research first. I promise it will pay off in the long run.

- Us ADHDers can be impulsive, and it isn't always easy to understand our own decision-making processes. An ADHD business coach can be invaluable and give you long-lasting strategies for success.

- Manifestations and affirmations are a great way to flip your mindset and put you in a more positive headspace. Give them a try!

Chapter 35

Fix You

> **Fix You *by Coldplay – from their album X&Y***
>
> This song reminds me of my husband's support during my darkest times. He helped me, but my ADHD diagnosis helped me heal myself – I wasn't broken, just different.

I was making progress. I felt as though I had found my community of people on *TikTok*, but then I started to doubt my diagnosis. The place I'd been diagnosed (the one I said was cheap) went bust. At around the same time, *Panorama* released a documentary about ADHD being over-diagnosed.

What if I'd been misdiagnosed? I'd be a fraud! I joined the NHS waiting list, but was told that it would take about four years to get a diagnosis. Luckily though, I'd learnt about Right to Choose (thanks to my *TikTok* rabbit hole) and told my doctors to refer me through this pathway, which I talked about in Chapter 33. In the UK, it's a route to a faster diagnosis.

My doctors didn't know what Right to Choose was – don't be disheartened if you experience something similar. I told mine that they were the professionals and that they should investigate! By February 2023, I was on the waiting list, and by September that year, I had my forms to fill in.

These forms need to be completed by people who have known you for a long time. Only after you submit the forms will you be invited for an assessment. I asked Rach, my friend of 30 years, and James, who is about the only person who knows me better than she does.

Rach was a bit worried though, 'I don't want you to be offended by what I've said', she told me.

'Why would I be offended?' I asked.

'Because I basically said you were awful at everything!' she told me. I laughed – I was super grateful and not at all offended.

James found the process eye-opening, and I think it helped him understand me better, even though he'd already started learning about ADHD after my private diagnosis.

The form I had to fill in asked questions like:

- Do you struggle to pay attention when something is boring?

- Do you often squirm about in your seat or walk around?

- Do you interrupt people when they are talking?

Errrm, yes to all of them! Interrupting is probably my worst trait – I don't do it to be rude, I just get super excited because of the way my brain processes things. If I think I know what you're going to say, I blurt stuff out and interrupt. I struggle to wait my turn in all situations.

I had decided that once I had my diagnosis, I would try and get medication. Despite now having two new businesses, I was still struggling with my mental health and with debt. That said, I wasn't stressed about the debt this time around. Because it was business debt, it felt different to when I was younger. Even though I still owed a lot of money, I was paying it off in little chunks and business creditors seemed more understanding.

My priority was to pay it off and get on with my life. I wasn't even worried about my credit score.

MOMENT OF TRUTH

I finally got my assessment date. The psychiatrist I spoke to was patient and professional. In the 90-minute call, she asked me lots of questions and for

my childhood evidence. I had a list of everything
I struggled with, and I read her some extracts from my
school reports.

'Have you thought about autism?' she asked.

'Erm, thought what about autism?' I replied.

'That you most likely have it, often it co-exists with
ADHD', she explained.

What the fresh merry hell* was she on about! I didn't
have autism! No way!! Of course, I went straight to
TikTok and researched.

Here are the main autism traits I uncovered:

- Struggles to maintain relationships
- Sensory issues with food, clothing and
  environment
- Self-harming behaviours
- Fixations on people, foods and activities
- Struggles with regulating emotions
- Struggles with bright lights and loud noises
- Struggles with social cues
- Struggles with overstimulation

FFS another one? There were lots of crossovers
with ADHD, but I resonated with every single
symptom.

At the end of the ADHD assessment, my psychiatrist said, 'I have never seen anyone present their ADHD symptoms as ADHD-ly as you'. Her comments were a resounding, 'Yes Maddy, you have ADHD'. I wasn't surprised, but I was really relieved that for the last year I hadn't been making it up and telling people I had it for no reason.

I scored 13/13 and was diagnosed with combined-type ADHD.

I was put on the list for titration, but was told it would be another three to four months before I could get access to medication. Why do they make processes such a hasslefest* for neurodivergent people?

How Do People Feel After They Have an ADHD Diagnosis?

Kim Raine, ADHD Performance Coach (kimrainecoaching.com), has shared some great insights into how it can feel after you receive an ADHD diagnosis.

I have coached several clients through diagnosis, both one-to-one and in the ABC, as well as some from realisation to diagnosis. I have seen them before and after, and the change is phenomenal. There is still work to do but it does make a huge difference to their confidence and the way they show up in their lives and businesses.

(continued)

- **Validation:** You're not crazy or lazy; ADHD is a structural brain difference, not a personal failing.

- **Self-compassion:** Missed deadlines or forgotten tasks aren't character flaws, just ADHD challenges.

- **Grief:** Mourn what undiagnosed ADHD cost you, then move forward using your strengths.

- **Anger:** Feeling frustrated about a late diagnosis is valid, but acceptance frees you to move on.

- **Self-awareness:** Understanding your brain helps you adjust routines, environments and relationships.

- **Empowerment:** Thriving starts when you work with your brain, not against it.

So, do I think getting an ADHD diagnosis is worth it?

HELL YES! It's been game changing for me, and I feel so much more in control, now that I understand my brain.

It's important to point out that there are three types of ADHD.

Types of ADHD
Inattentive ADHD

Traits include but are not limited to

- Difficulty paying attention or concentrating.

- Getting easily distracted (oh, a squirrel).

- Losing things on a regular basis like your keys or phone (most of the time, they are in your hand).

- Struggling to follow simple instructions (have you ever tried to build Lego?!).

- Forgetting dates or double-booking.

- Avoiding tasks you dislike, especially ones that require brain power.

- Zoning out when people speak to you.

Hyperactive/Impulsive ADHD

- Fidgeting or squirming.

- Constant brain activity (like you have lots of things going on at once).

- Feeling restless and not able to sit still.

- Interrupting or blurting out things without being in control.

- Difficulty waiting in line or waiting your turn (queuing sucks!).

- Risky and impulsive behaviours (like overspending, gambling, drinking too much).

(continued)

Combined-Type ADHD

A combination of the two, which is the beautiful variety that I have! Apparently, girls and women are more likely to have inattentive type, but most of the women I know seem to have both.

It's important to understand that hyperactivity doesn't have to be visible; if you feel like you are driven by a motor or that your brain is constantly loud, that also counts.

FINDING ADDITIONAL SUPPORT

After getting my second, more official, diagnosis, I heard about *Access to Work*, which was a government grant to help to support employed and self-employed people in the UK to stay in work.

Apply for an *Access To Work* Grant

The UK government offers *Access to Work* grants, which are designed to help those with neurodivergent conditions, disabilities or anything else that impacts your day-to-day life in the workplace or as a business owner, and this money can be used to support your business.

You can apply for one of these grants whether you are employed, self-employed or an entrepreneur. To apply, you need to identify the condition you have and how it impacts you in the workplace.

I'm not going to lie to you, it's a complete hasslefest* to apply for – I'm talking forms, questionnaires, calls and a tonne of planning – I've put together a video walkthrough of what you need to do on my Stan Store to help, you can use it as a body-double to help you to apply. And just in case any of the press are reading this I am going to clarify! This is for people who are struggling with their condition, it is not for people to try and buck the system or defraud the government. #sickfluencer (can you see me rolling my eyes)

As an ADHD entrepreneur, I think one of the best ways to use the grant is to invest in a virtual assistant who can help you with time management, admin, emails and diary management.

I applied and was granted some money to help me in my business, which was totally life-changing for me. Being able to get someone to help me with day-to-day admin and processes – like blogs and sales funnels – meant that I could focus on my business and do the things I love, which mainly consisted of social media, sales and coaching.

It also allowed me to invest in some coaching for myself, which turned out to be incredibly helpful, and gave me an idea of an area I should place more focus on – ADHD coaching.

I started to investigate ADHD coaching courses and found an amazing company to train with, called *Thrive*.

I didn't really need the coaching qualification. I had done a coaching qualification earlier in my career, but I needed to become more familiar with ADHD. So, I became a neurodiversity in the workplace trainer. After the way I had been treated in jobs previously, and now knowing about how my brain is different, this was something I felt really passionate about.

I hyperfocused and passed my neurodiversity qualification, which means I now work with corporates, mainly banks and fintech companies, to help them to be more inclusive with their employees and their customers.

During this course, I learned even more than I already knew about neurodiversity and all of the neurodivergent conditions.

A NEW LEVEL OF UNDERSTANDING

I realised that I have the full fruit bowl – even very mild Tourette's. I click my tongue on the roof of my mouth, and I have a shoulder twitch, which I just thought were things I did out of boredom, but it turns out when you are really aware of something you notice it more and I don't notice I'm doing it half the time. I am really lucky that it doesn't interfere with my life.

As I mentioned in the Preface, I also have dyslexia, dyspraxia, dyscalculia and dysgraphia. The dyslexia I was aware of, but the others I had no idea about.

Some of the signs of dyspraxia are the same as those for ADHD, like being highly distractible and having difficulty concentrating for long periods of time. Another sign of dyspraxia is difficulty retaining information – this was me all over. I always found exams and revision really hard, and it was probably why I didn't do as well as I could have at school.

Difficulty with spatial awareness is another sign of dyspraxia. I am always bumping into things, I trip over thin air, I fall up and down stairs and even miss my mouth with food and drink. It also means I think I have more space than I do when driving, so I often reverse into things or bang into gateposts. Not knowing my left from my right is another element of this.

Dyscalculia means you struggle with numbers. I was terrible at maths when I was younger, and I even find it a struggle to record my money in spreadsheets. I find it works better for my brain to write the figures down in a notepad – seeing numbers there is easier and the physical act of writing them helps my memory.

But dyscalculia also shows up with signs like getting lost easily – massive tick for that one – and difficulty telling the time. It also makes understanding sequences much more challenging.

I remember that as a child I couldn't look at stuff like the periodic table or learn my times tables. As I mentioned earlier, I always found songs and music helped me with this. My daughter Harriet is the same – she learns best through sound. You have to find what works for you and your kids and roll with it.

Although I have dysgraphia, I only struggle with this a bit. Some of the signs of dysgraphia – like spelling and punctuation errors – could come down to my dyslexia. Other signs of dysgraphia are illegible handwriting, difficulty gripping a pen (if you get hand cramp while using a pen, this could be why!), not being able to write within lines and writing on a slant.

Most of my homework as a kid looked like I had written it upside down whilst rolling down a hill.

Just knowing I have these conditions makes it so much easier to put stuff in place to support myself. I think being aware, even if you don't get diagnosed, really helps.

My other advice to you is not to let anyone fob you off. If you think that you have a neurodivergent condition, then own it. The more we talk about these things and the way they affect us, the more people will learn and respect us and our crazy, different and beautiful brains.

The more I looked into all of my neurodivergent conditions, the more I realised I had spent most of my life masking. This means you pretend you are OK with certain situations when you aren't. For example, making eye contact always makes me feel uncomfortable and you get told you have to do it.

Another example is hugging people when you don't want to. I am fine with hugging on my terms, but let me instigate it!

Masking for me also meant dulling down my personality to be less 'weird' or 'quirky', mimicking people's social behaviour to fit in and rehearsing conversations so you don't say the wrong thing.

ANOTHER REALISATION...

After 12 weeks of waiting my titration process started. Taking ADHD meds is game changing. It's not going to be for everyone, but for me it has been life-altering in a good way.

I remember the first few weeks so clearly. The medication, to my surprise, actually made my mind clear. I used to describe my brain as being like a Sky TV with a million channels all playing at once and no remote to turn them off. The medication was my remote.

Suddenly, I only had one train of thought. It was just my inner monologue – the rest of the channels were silent. In truth, I think this is the first time I had ever really heard silence (if you can hear it?!), and it was extremely weird.

However, one of the biggest changes I noticed was that my senses were all over the place. For instance, the clothes I'd been wearing for the last two years, like my favourite jumper, felt like they were full of stinging nettles and irritating beyond belief.

I also wasn't enjoying social situations as much, which made me drink more because I felt uncomfortable. God forbid anyone touched me! I couldn't cope with sounds or bright lights – I ended up wearing sunglasses to one gig where there were flashing lights and looked like a right tit.

Textures, tastes and smells were also a source of sensitivity. My ADHD meds had got rid of my anxiety and I felt like a totally new person but there, clear as day, were all my autistic symptoms. With my ADHD 'removed', it revealed that my autism had been hiding underneath all along.

When the psychiatrist had first told me she thought I might have autism, I had refused to believe it. But my ADHD meds had taken that mask off and I had another piece of fruit* to add to the bowl.

Things to Consider When Seeking Diagnosis

- Think about why you are looking to get diagnosed, whether it is for validation, or to get medication or additional support. Understanding your own 'why' will help you to better advocate for yourself.

- Do your research.

- Look for professionals who can help and guide you.

- Think about whether you want to go down the private or NHS route (if in the UK). Private can come with additional challenges and difficulties in getting medication, but NHS can often take longer.

- Write down your symptoms so you are prepared. If it helps, watch some of my *TikTok* videos; I am sure they will help you to pick out some symptoms.

- Speak to your family; this can be hard, but they may have supporting evidence from your childhood.

- Remember that women present ADHD in a different way to men; we often mask, and our symptoms can be more internal than external.

- Be ready to champion yourself; you know your brain better than anyone else.

- Remember there are three types of ADHD: hyperactive/impulsive and inattentive, or combined, which is a combination of the two.

BECOMING VISIBLE

I felt a weird sense of grief, like I was mourning for the life I could have had. It felt weird knowing I had had these conditions all of my life and never known about them. Would I have avoided getting so badly into debt had I known? I guess we will never know, but knowledge is power, and I can use this knowledge to help me now.

Although the autism made me even more quirky than I already was, I felt weirdly relieved and was happy to lean into my weird. I had always been weird, and I could finally take off the suit I had been wearing and fully be myself. I was not invisible anymore.

Autism isn't something you can treat, so you just have to learn how it affects you and how the symptoms present themselves. Every single person with autism on this planet has different signs because we all have different brains.

Similarly, we all have different ways of describing our neurodivergent conditions.

I used to hate the term 'neurospicy', because I felt like it was almost mocking and making something pretty serious sound fun and fluffy. Don't get me started on 'neurosparkly' and 'neurospangly', either. But if you want to use any of those to describe you, that's your call. There is a lot of shade that gets thrown for how people describe themselves, and I think it's cool if you have a condition to identify with whatever word you want to for it, especially if it helps you to process it.

As you might have noticed, my preference is to say I have a fruit bowl of neurodivergent conditions.

I wish there were neurodivergent pronouns, like we have for gender, so we could each say how we identify. Maybe that's a campaign for the future. In all seriousness though, I think it would be amazing if we could put our neurodiverse or invisible conditions on display on our LinkedIn profiles. We should be able to wear them with honour and not feel ashamed.

While I was writing this book, I recorded a *TikTok* about having a panic attack on a train. I was wearing the hidden disabilities sunflower lanyard, which shows others that I have a hidden disability. Everyone on the train was so lovely that they found me a seat, offered me water and checked in on me.

I'm not sure that would have happened if I hadn't been wearing the sunflower lanyard. It would be nice if we could get to a point where people don't judge those who wear the sunflower lanyard. You can learn more about sunflower lanyards here: `https://hdsunflower.com`

When it comes to how we describe ourselves, I say I'm an ADHD-er or I have autism. I haven't quite got my head around the AuDHD label yet, but I guess this is what I am, among other things. Actually, I think I'm AUDHDDDDPMDDHASHI – Menopausal. Yeah, let's go with that!

 Gems of Wisdom

- Whether you choose to get a diagnosis is a personal thing, but in my experience, it is overwhelmingly positive and helps you access more support.

(continued)

- ADHD is often associated with other conditions – like autism, dyspraxia, dyslexia, dyscalculia and dysgraphia. Finding out all of that can be overwhelming, so take your time to process your diagnosis however you need to.
- There is support available, so speak to someone like me or do your own research to find out what's out there that could help you.

Chapter 36

Maybe

It's important to know that when you first discover you have ADHD, you may feel a sense of loss, grief or imposter syndrome. You might feel like you don't know who you are anymore or what your purpose is on this planet. That is totally normal. You can also feel relieved, happy and want to celebrate. It can also make you feel exhausted.

All of the emotions you feel when you are diagnosed are totally valid. But it doesn't make them any less confusing.

My biggest advice to anyone newly diagnosed is, *be kind to yourself*. Don't blame yourself, or your parents, just accept and learn. Try not to be angry with the world. Society didn't help us, and neither did the doctors, especially those with a late diagnosis. Remember it's only relatively recently that neurodivergent conditions have become a more common topic of conversation, and that many have been identified in women.

Society now is helping us to discover who we are and also allowing us to understand our children more. We just need to learn and educate others. The more we talk about it, the more we will be accepted and supported.

A CONSTANT LEARNING JOURNEY

I was learning more about my brain every day. Some of it was horrendous, but there were also some really good bits. I liked what I could see so far, but something was still massively masking who I was, and it needed to go: alcohol.

As you know, I could be described as a semi-professional drinker in my 20s. I was also an incredibly irresponsible drinker and got myself into some really sticky situations as a result. I had no self-control – that famous missing off switch.

Drinking was fun until it wasn't. Most people have the ability to realise that they are pissed, stop drinking and remove themselves from the situation. I didn't. If I felt pissed, I would see how far I could push myself.

An incredibly boozy night in January 2024 made me realise I'm not in my 20s anymore and can no longer hold my booze. Having kids meant I'd stopped drinking as often, but when I did have a drink I'd binge, trying to cram a year's worth of drinking into one night.

I realised that I drank because it made me feel 'normal'. I also realised that I couldn't be 'normal' if I tried. I was using alcohol to give myself confidence in social situations, but the reality was that I was making a massive tit out of myself and spending way more money than I needed to by trying to keep up with friends.

I started to say no to shots. They were the thing that made me go from merry pissed to completely slaughtered. That was fairly easy. Even though I was scared of saying no when shots were offered, in case people thought I was weird, I could hide them or dump them in the nearest flowerpot.

My friends have always been big drinkers, and I used to be really comfortable with it, but I was no longer comfortable. My hangovers were lasting for days, and my mental health wasn't good. I noticed that when I got drunk on a weekend, I was actually really low and unproductive for the whole week after. I cut down the amount I was drinking. Alcohol needed to go in the 'fuck-it bucket'*.

ALL OR NOTHING

I think I have always been an all-or-nothing sort of girl, so I decided it had to be nothing, for a while at least.

I finally gave up smoking after on–off smoking for nearly 20 years. It wasn't that hard to stop, and I had to think of the kids. I was careful not to smoke in front of them, but the number of times I'd 'put the bins out' a day was a dead giveaway.

Smoking and drinking went hand in hand. Once I had stopped smoking, the drinking part was easier. My biggest tip for anyone who wants to give something up – whatever addiction it is – is to **not** tell yourself you can never have it again. I knew that if I wanted alcohol again, then it was there. This didn't have to be 'forever'.

I also told people that I was stopping drinking. It made social situations easier, and I would drive to as many things as I could as a way of not being tempted.

I started to push myself to attend things that would usually be boozy for me, like festivals. I did Slam Dunk Festival sober for the first time ever, and it was amazing! I remembered every single band I saw. The highlight for me was RØRY – Rox is not only an incredible artist and performer but also one of my favourite

ADHD content creators. She inspired me to
try sobriety.

I never considered myself an alcoholic, but I was
someone who used booze as a crutch. Getting rid of
that crutch made me hobble for a bit. It was weird
going to gigs sober initially, but now it's great.

Weddings felt like they'd also be a challenge, but
I went to my friend Amy's wedding where I knew
nobody and I stayed sober, and I had the best time.

Watching rugby was probably the hardest, but the first
time I watched the Roses play sober, I found that
I enjoyed the sport way more and remembered
the match.

Drinking masked my ADHD and autism, I wasn't
myself. Learning to be more me and live with my fruit
bowl of neurodivergent conditions actually meant that
I had to know who I was without the booze. I also
found that booze would cause a flare-up of my
Hashimoto's, sometimes lasting weeks.

It hasn't been easy, but it's been the best thing for
my mental health. My Hashimoto's thanks me,
my kids thank me for being more present, and
the more I go out now the more I realise I am still the
life of the party. I don't need booze to have a good
time, and the impact on my business from both stopping drinking and being on meds has been
game changing.

I am still allowing myself to drink if I want to, but my new rule is that I can't get drunk, **ever**!

When I went to the Isle of Wight Festival in 2024, I had four alcoholic drinks over the whole weekend. This just proved even further that I didn't need booze. I didn't see this as falling off the wagon, it merely reinforced my belief that alcohol doesn't work for me.

I don't say I am 'sober'; it took a conversation with the lovely Suzanne Shaw about how not drinking and being alcohol-free doesn't mean you never have to drink again, to realise it isn't black and white.

I know I won't ever be a drinker again. But the odd sip won't kill me. You just have to understand your own triggers. So don't have any if you know it's a trigger for you.

I have my own path, and what works for me won't work for others. But allowing myself to drink alcohol if I want to has helped me to cut it out totally. The next addiction to tackle is sugar, but I'm not sure I can do that yet.

Why Alcohol Is Not Great for ADHDers

First, this comes from a place of love, not judgement. But these are some of the reasons why I think not drinking when you have ADHD is probably a good idea.

(continued)

- **Dopamine trap:** We chase the high and don't know when to stop, leading to risky situations.

- **Addiction risk:** Dopamine makes booze hard to resist (as my own journey proves).

- **Mental health hit:** Hangxiety, mood swings and nervous system dysregulation, especially in perimenopause.

- **Expensive habit:** Quitting saves on drinks, taxis and takeaways.

- **Poor judgement:** Alcohol fuels risky decisions, leading to regret.

- **Medication interference:** It can weaken or worsen effects.

- **Ruins sleep:** ADHD brains *really* need good sleep to function.

I am learning who I am without the booze and, to be honest, I love what I see. I am proud of myself, and that I have changed my relationship with booze. I vow to never have a hangover ever again and I can see that actually being a future for me.

Sadly, it hasn't changed my weight. I'm still on the cuddly side, but I am also coming to terms with the fact that it's bloody hard to lose weight when you have an autoimmune disease, and I am beginning to be proud of my curves and celebrate my body for what it is.

I also worked out that, since I stopped drinking, I have saved over £2,000. This is not just spending on booze but on things like taxis, crap hangover takeaways, ADHD tax! I'm a very generous person when it comes to buying stuff for people, so it helped me to save there as well. Not to mention the number of impulse purchases that I made whilst under the influence of alcohol is just insane! I could probably write a book just about that!

Since stopping drinking, I have become more of a present mum, and I have more energy to do things with the kids. I do more activities with them, I read more to them, and we go out for walks and to the beach. They are so much happier, and that makes me happy.

 Gems of Wisdom

- When you receive a diagnosis of any kind of neurodivergent condition, you set out on a learning journey. Embrace it and see where it takes you, there is loads you can learn that will benefit your life.
- Booze often doesn't go well with ADHD. I'm not here to tell you whether or not to drink alcohol, but I can share that cutting it out has had a massive positive impact on my life.

Chapter 37

Overcome

Overcome *by Nothing but Thieves – from their album* Dead Club City

This was my 2024 hyperfocus song – the one that made me notice Nothing but Thieves. It's all about resilience, change, compromise and pushing forward.

I went into 2024 with a new qualification as a neurodiversity specialist, and my coaching was really taking off. I was starting to build a community of amazing neurodivergent entrepreneurs and business owners around me, and helping them change their money stories too.

By the time February came around, I understood so much more about my own brain and my condition. I was talking more openly on my *TikTok* channel *madaboutmoneyofficial* about my life and how my conditions affected me.

But I wasn't just talking about ADHD anymore. I was talking about all of my hidden disabilities.

I got a blue tick on *TikTok* as a verified person, which was great but also kind of annoying because I couldn't change my handle to encompass more than just money. I wanted to talk about my business journey, my life and to tell more of my story to help other people.

Money is, and will always be, part of my story. I still want to help as many people as I can to change their money story. But I also want to help people who have businesses. I have run businesses for the last eight years, and it's so evident to me that my businesses being successful means that I have to work with my brain not against it.

I started a membership programme for entrepreneurs to help them to become more visible in their business. It's called *Invisible to Influential*. I used what I had learned in *One to Many* to put my processes and launch into play. I started with a soft launch and got 220 people into my membership, which was not only making me a semi-passive income every day but also giving me so much joy!

I was helping people to apply for *Access to Work* for their businesses and helping them to get the support they need to actually make money in their business. I realised I had found my calling: helping entrepreneurs with hidden disabilities to get more money into their businesses; helping people to become proud of their conditions and get more visible on social media; and helping people to be the go-to expert in their niche. We all need to be influential, no matter what business we run.

As the year went on, I had even more people coming to me for support, and *TikTok* training for their groups. I was also getting asked to speak about neurodiversity and money for corporate companies, as well as speaking at money festivals and events.

Still no TEDx – I'm working on that for this year. But I had found my purpose, and I felt so alive.

Advice to Connect with Your Inner Self and Purpose

Victoria Dioh, African Oracle (Intuit and Healer) at www.victoriadioh.com, has some great advice to help you connect to yourself and feel into whether you're on the right path.

First, choose a calming word. Pick a word that instantly helps you feel calm – something simple,

(continued)

like the word 'calm' or even the name of your pet! Write this word down somewhere where you can see it daily, like on a Post-it or in your planner.

When you're feeling hyper, scattered or overwhelmed, look at your calming word and take a deep breath. The word acts as an anchor to help ground you. Every time you get caught in a wave of excitement or stress, pause and tap into that word. You'll start to feel your energy shift, allowing you to refocus.

By using this method consistently, you'll be able to train your mind to respond to the word as a trigger for calm, helping you regain control in moments of overwhelm. Think of this word before you try any of the following exercises.

Tune into your energy: Notice when tasks energise or drain you. Explore, don't quit.

Trust your gut: Pause and listen to how decisions feel in your body.

Embrace hyperfocus: Your flow state may reveal your true purpose. Jot down what excites you.

Set intentions, not strict plans: Blend intuition with logic for flexible structure.

Follow joy: ADHD thrives on excitement; small bursts of joy signal alignment.

> **Spot patterns:** Notice when things effortlessly fall into place.
>
> **Seek calm:** Moments of clarity amid ADHD chaos are signs you're on track.

MOVING FORWARD WITH POSITIVITY

I trained as a business strategist as well, so I can help more people with invisible conditions with their business strategies. I want people to know that they don't have to be limited by their condition or past traumas.

In typical ADHD style, I did the whole eight-week course in two days, and the exam and case study in a morning. And I passed it!

I still have debt from My VIP Card, but I'm chipping away at it gradually and I have a plan to clear more this year. In fact, if all goes well, by the time you're reading this book, I will be debt-free once more, and I won't ever go back to being in scary debt again.

Of course, I didn't plan to get into debt the second time, but damn you ADHD, sometimes it does get in my way.

I am working with my kids to understand more about them and their brains, whilst talking about ADHD and autism with them most days. I want them to understand that they are different, mummy is different and that is OK.

I have had over a year without being drunk, which is a massive win for me! In fact, I can count on one hand the number of alcoholic drinks I have had. Stopping drinking has been pretty game changing, and I know that I will never go back to drinking the way I did before.

Mentally, I'm feeling the strongest and most positive I ever have done. I think the meds are really helping with that, but so is my mindset. I am feeling more positive about life.

I feel like I am winning and have found my community. I am a happier parent and a better person because of everything I have been through. I highly suspect it won't be the last time I go through stuff, but I am now going into life understanding my brain and also understanding others.

One of the biggest things I learned through this process was that I was scared of being successful. Not being successful kept me safe. I had success earlier too, and it led to me being in the worst place mentally health-wise. I had imposter syndrome. My mental monologue was full of questions like, who was I to be able to be successful? What if people didn't like me anymore when I became successful? I don't like change, what if I became too successful? Now I take the Cassie Phillips (yeah Mel Robbins didn't invent this!) approach of 'Let them'; I do what is right for me and my family and the people I care about.

The thing is, if you do it slowly, take every day as it comes and push one step forward every day, people will grow with you. Being successful is not an overnight thing, you have to work at it – and if you have the right strategies in place for your mind and your business, then you can be successful. You just need to get out of your own way.

I have got a successful business. I am hitting and exceeding my goals. I am happy with the direction my business is taking me in. I'm working with some amazing entrepreneurs who have hidden disabilities to help them to thrive.

I finally feel like I have found my place. No more job hopping or changing my mind about what I do every day. Oh, and I have made over £100k this year in my business! Just through being super visible!

I still get a million business ideas, but I share them with my clients to help them to have better businesses. I am collaborating with some amazing people. When you work together, great things happen.

I hate all the 'teamwork makes the dream work' BS, but it really does help you to grow.

LOOKING TO THE FUTURE

What is next for me? I want to carry on championing those with invisible conditions and helping them to be better with money and business. I will carry on telling my story. I expect there will be a second book because I have so much to talk about.

And I want to talk more about how telling my story has made me so visible – maybe *Invisible to Influential* should be the next book. Let me know if you want another one!

It feels a bit like an anti-climax leaving the book here, so I want to tell you that I am the happiest I have been in a very long time.

I have the best friendship group I could ever ask for, as well as the best and most supportive husband who is constantly learning about my neurodivergent conditions so he can support me in the best ways.

My mum and I are still great friends, my dad and I have repaired our once-fragile relationship.

My membership is my happy place, I love my members and helping them to be more visible is my calling.

I created the most inclusive and crazy online event in my online world "The Maddyverse" called Visible Fest, it would be awesome to see some of you at the next one!

My parting words to you all:

Don't let your ADHD, or whatever other conditions you may have, stop you from sorting your money out, growing a successful business or

showing up as you. Be bold, be brave and be unstoppable.

- The only person standing in your way is you. You can take on the world.

- If I can turn my life around as a walking disaster zone*, you guys can too.

- Remember you are not bad with money or bad at business, you have ADHD!!

- You don't need a diagnosis to start understanding who you are, regardless of what conditions you may have. The more you learn about your brain and your body, the more you can succeed in life. Work with it not against it.

- Mindset is one of the most important things, it can change your money story and your business story. As Henry Ford once famously said, 'Whether you believe you can or you believe you can't, you are right'.

You can change your money story. So why not start here?

So much love to you all, and thank you so much for buying this book, it means the world to me. Give me a follow on whatever platform you hang out on most – I am everywhere! And make sure you check out all of the freebies in my Stan Store!

Maddy xxx

Resources

How you can work with me . . .

- ☐ Mad About Money app: This can be downloaded from app stores for free. You'll get access to me and my business partner Vix to help change your money story.

- ☐ You can join Invisible to Influential my membership for entrepreneurs at `maddyalexander grout.com`. It will help you with visibility and business strategy.

- ☐ If you want to work with me one-to-one, you can either do that through Access To Work (I accept Access to Work funding) or direct, just follow me on TikTok @madaboutmoneyofficial.

- ☐ I run online and in-person events called Visible Fest.

- ☐ If this book has helped you in any way, please tell your friends about it.

The following resources are ones that I've found useful in the UK. Wherever you are in the world, there will likely be similar support available, so do
your research:

Action on Postpartum Psychosis: `https://www.app-network.org/`

Pandas Foundation for postnatal awareness and support: `https://pandasfoundation.org.uk/`

National Autistic Society, advice about PDA: `https://www.autism.org.uk/advice-and-guidance/topics/behaviour/demand-avoidance`

The Complaining Cow, information about the Consumer Rights Act 2015: `https://thecomplainingcow.co.uk/a-guide-to-the-consumer-rights-act-2015/`

The Complaining Cow, information about using an ombudsman to settle disputes: `https://www.thecomplainingcow.co.uk/alternative-dispute-resolution-what-it-all-means/%20/o%20The%20ADR%20Directive%20and%20Ombudsman%20Omnishambles`

The Complaining Cow, information about small claims court: `https://www.thecomplainingcow.co.uk/the-small-claims-court-process-made-simple/%20/t%20_blank`

Step Change UK debt advice charity: `https://www`
`.stepchange.org/`

`Totallymoney.com` for free tips on how to improve
your credit score.

Loqbox for saving and improving your credit score.

Transfermybills app for admin support when
moving home.

Dubbii app to help hold you accountable: `https://`
`www.adhd-love.co.uk/`

The F**k: Glossary

Another piece of fruit to put in the bowl – another f*cking condition I didn't know I had.

Catastrophuk – when a minor issue snowballs into a full-blown f*cking crisis.

Chaos conductor – when it feels like everything you touch turns into a f*cking mess, and you're somehow orchestrating mishap after mishap. Life's little disasters, starring you as the main f*cking character.

Disasterbait – catastrophize the f*ck out of any situation that feels overwhelming or unpleasant.

Doodlefart – a complete brain meltdown and instead of doing something useful, you just f*cking doodle.

Dopamine lull – a f*cking relief that the pressure is over but the sudden loss of purpose makes you feel like complete f*cking shit.

Drink for England – getting so f*cking drunk that I could have tried to text my ex's tortoise and wondered why they didn't reply.

FITT – the best-looking man I'd ever seen.

Flip the script – f*ck this shit, I'm changing my life.

Fluffed up – f*cked up.

Flusterblast – f*cking overwhelming blast of fury.

Foot-in-mouth disease – saying something without thinking that comes back to bite you in the arse. A massive f*cking embarrassment that's self-inflicted by your mouth activating before your brain.

For flump's sake – for f*ck's sake

F*ck it bucket – a place you put things (physical or mental) that are never seen or heard of again. This could be a bin, a drawer or a mental compartment. Example: chuck it in the f*ck it bucket.

Fuzzled up – f*cked up.

Fuzz – f*ck!!

Hasslefest – a real f*cking ballache.

High-speed bathroom shuffle – when things are moving way too fast and you're in a panicked dash to make it. If you don't get to the toilet in the next three seconds you're going to f*cking shit yourself.

Instant terror surge – f*cking freaked out.

Mother Hubbard – motherf*cker.

No freaking way – also known as no f*cking way.

Nope, not playing that game – f*ck this for a game of soldiers. Something that is a waste of time, effort or patience until you're absolutely f*cking done with it.

Ouchy – really f*cking hurts, but not in a 'f*ck me this is uncomfortable' way like a smear test, or in a 'f*ck me I'm dying' way like giving birth. Just f*cking ouchy.

Peopled out – f*cking done with any human interaction for the day and I just want to doom scroll my phone.

Permanent oops mode – when it feels like life is one long series of 'Oops' moments. Every time you try to get it right, something goes hilariously f*cking wrong.

Procrastifaffing – stop f*cking thinking, start f*cking doing.

Professional misstepper – you're unintentionally a pro at f*cking things up, no matter how good your intentions. F*cking things up feels like part of the job description.

Really blooming employable – shit hot at what I f*cking do.

Rhino in – being like a bull in a f*cking china shop and not analysing the situation before opening your mouth.

Saucepan of poopoo – crock of f*cking shit.

Serial blunderer – when you feel like you're constantly stumbling from one mistake to the next, like it's become your unintentional specialty. The art of f*cking up, on repeat.

Spilling tea that's all about me – talking shit about me.

Stubborn as a mule on caffeine – stubborn as f*ck. I'm literally not doing it unless I think it's my f*cking idea.

Suggestive with the eyes – flirty as f*ck.

Tapped out – f*cking done with everything and I just want to hide under my duvet and binge watch Netflix.

Totally Baltic – aka so f*cking freezing I felt like my boobs might fall off.

Totally bricking it – shit f*cking scared.

Walking disaster zone – when you feel like a human tornado, leaving a trail of accidental f*ck ups every-where you go. If there's a way to f*ck it up, you'll find it.

What the fresh merry hell . . . – what the f*ck . . .

What in the world of wizardry is going on? – what the f*ck is going on?

Wiggle jiggle break – when your ADHD is so f*cking trapped that you have an overwhelming desire to get up and move, and you have to do it at all costs.

About the Author

Maddy Alexander-Grout is a dynamic visibility strategist, ADHD coach and money specialist. She is on a mission to empower individuals with ADHD, other neurodivergent conditions and hidden struggles to achieve financial confidence and personal visibility.

Through her relatable style, Maddy has built a successful business by sharing her journey of how she went from £40,000 of debt to financial security. She understands first-hand the unique challenges faced by neurodivergent individuals, having experienced the overwhelm, impulsivity and financial missteps that often come with ADHD.

Named as one of the Shaw Trust Disability Power 100 in November 2024, Maddy is recognised as a leading voice in her field. She frequently appears in the press and hosts her own podcast, **Mad About Money,** where she discusses visibility, vulnerability and resilience with guests.

Her story is one of resilience and growth, proving that it's possible to turn vulnerability into influence and financial strength. Through her work, Maddy champions authenticity, empowering her audience to embrace their unique journeys.

When she's not guiding others to financial freedom, Maddy enjoys spending time with her family, going to gigs and festivals and binge-watching Netflix whenever she has time.

Index

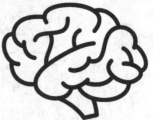

ALCOHOL switches off MY ADHD. BUT MY ADHD has no off switch WHEN IT COMES TO ALCOHOL

ADHD isn't a flaw
It's a part of my personality

You are not a
BROKEN HORSE
You are a
beautiful
RAINBOW
ZEBRA

having an ADHD brain is like TRYING TO PLAY A CASSETTE TAPE IN A CD PLAYER

YOU ARE NOT

BAD WITH MONEY or

BAD AT BUSINESS

You have

ADHD